Totally SPRING

Edited by
Sherrill B. Flora

Publishers
T.S. Denison & Company, Inc.
Minneapolis, Minnesota 55431

Some of the material has been compiled from *The Preschool Papers* - Sept. 1987 through Summer 1989, written by Sherrill B. Flora.

Standard Book Number: 513-01997-9
Totally Spring
Copyright © 1990 by T.S. Denison and Company, Inc.
Minneapolis, Minnesota 55431

CONTENTS

*HOLIDAY AND SEASONAL UNITS FOR CHILDREN
AGED PRESCHOOL THROUGH GRADE TWO*

MARCH WINDS APRIL SHOWERS

CONTENTS

WEATHER ACTIVITIES

CLOUDS

Take the children outdoors on a day where there are a lot of cumulus clouds in the sky. If the weather permits, have the children lie down and look at the clouds. Encourage them to name the objects they see in the clouds. Point out that children looking at the same cloud can see different things. After returning to the classroom, give each child a 9" x 12" sheet of white construction paper. Tell the children to tear the construction paper to make a cloud. Cover a bulletin board with blue paper. When the children have finished their "clouds," place them on the bulletin board.

Have the children take turns telling what they think the different paper "clouds" look like. Write what the children say under the clouds for a language experience lesson. Encourage individual creativity and imagination.

THE WIND

Have the children fold a 9" x 12" paper into a fan. *"The air is all around us"* might be printed on the fan. Staple the bottom closed and suggest that the children can fan themselves. Can the children feel that the air is all around us?

Listen to the sound made by an empty jar or large shell pressed against the ear. Air makes a sound. Fill the jar with water. Listen for a sound now that the air is all gone.

MAKING RAIN

Bring water in a tea kettle to a boiling point so that the steam is rising from the spout. Put ice cubes in a small saucepan. Hold the saucepan over the spout of the tea kettle, so the steam from the spout strikes the bottom and sides of the saucepan. The steam will cool and condense to form droplets of water on the outside of the pan. These droplets will collect and fall like rain falling from a cloud.

A NOTE OF CAUTION: This experiment should be closely supervised.

CLOUD DROPPED CEILING

This dropped ceiling will be an interesting room decoration during a unit on weather or the seasons.

You will need: white craft or butcher paper; cotton; staples; glue; wire, string, or nylon fishing line

What you do: Cut two identical shapes of an irregular form. Staple together three sides and glue cotton balls to both sides of the "envelope." Stuff the shape with crumbled paper. Staple the fourth side and suspend the cloud from the ceiling with lightweight wire, string or nylon fishing line. Attach the cloud to the ceiling from four or five points.

Also try painting the paper grey or black to form storm clouds. Hang several clouds from the ceiling so it looks like the sky. This is a good activity for children to work together in small groups.

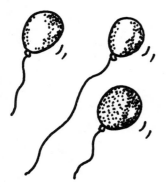

FLYING BALLOONS

Young children often find it difficult to fly a kite. Especially a kite made from construction paper. Children can have the experience of flying "something" other than a kite. Tie a string on the end of a balloon for each child. Let the children take their "balloon kites" outside and fly them. This is often a much more successful experience for a young child.

RAINBOW FRUIT SALAD

This is an easy and fun fruit salad made from all the colors in the rainbow; RED apples, ORANGE oranges, YELLOW bananas, GREEN grapes, BLUE blueberries, and PURPLE grapes. These are also all the fruits that children love to eat! Ask the children to name all the colors that they can find in their salads.

WIND AIRPLANE FUN

AIRPLANE FUN

• Have the children construct gliders from folded paper, then throw the gliders into the air. Explain that the gliders also depend on air to fly, but they don't work like jets do. The air under the gliders' wings makes them fly smoothly down to the ground instead of falling straight down.

• Make a balancing jet. Follow the pattern, cutting it out of thin cardboard. With tape, fasten pennies to the underside on the places marked. The pennies will make the little plane balance on the end of a pencil and you can walk around the room to make the jet "fly."

pennies

RHYMES/POETRY

THE WIND

The wind came out to play one day.
He swept the clouds out of his way;
   (make sweeping motions with arms)
He blew the leaves and away they flew.
   (make fluttering motions with fingers)
The trees bent low and their branches did, too.
   (lift arms and lower them)
The wind blew the great big ships at sea;
   (repeat sweeping motions)
The wind blew my kite away from me.

From, Rhymes for Fingers and Flannel Boards.
By Louise Binder Scott and J.J. Thompson.
Copyright © T.S. Denison & Co., Inc.

BLOWING BUBBLES

I like to blow bubbles,
   (puff out cheeks and blow)
And watch them fly.
Blue ones, purple ones,
Up in the sky.
   (look up)
Sometimes they pop!
   (blink eyes)
And get in my eyes.
   (rub eyes)
I blow them all over again,
   (blow again)
And I do not cry.
*(The month of March is a wonderful
time to take the children outside and
let them blow bubbles. The wind will
blow the bubbles "up & away" quickly.)*

WATCH THE RAINDROPS

I like to watch the raindrops
   Dancing in the street.
I like to jump in puddles
   With my little feet.

UMBRELLA

Here is my umbrella;
   (hold hands over head as an umbrella)
It will keep me dry.

When I go walking in the rain,
   (wiggle fingers in sprinkling motion)
I hold it up so high.
   (raise hand in the air)

RAIN, RAIN

Rain, rain,
Go away.
Come again
Another day;
Little Johnny
Wants to play.
*(Although this is
a fun poem to say,
we know that rain
is really helpful.
How?)*

Make a List

Make a list of all the activities you like to do when it is raining outside.

Name _____

Weather and Clothing

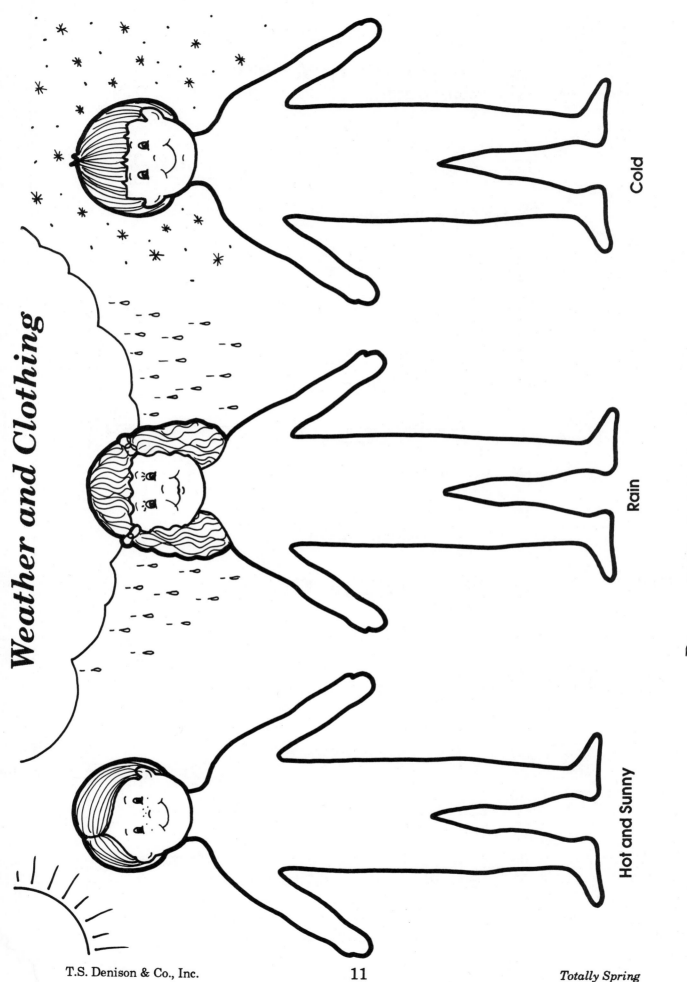

Cold

Rain

Hot and Sunny

Draw suitable clothing for each child.

WEATHER MUSIC ACTIVITIES

THE WIND

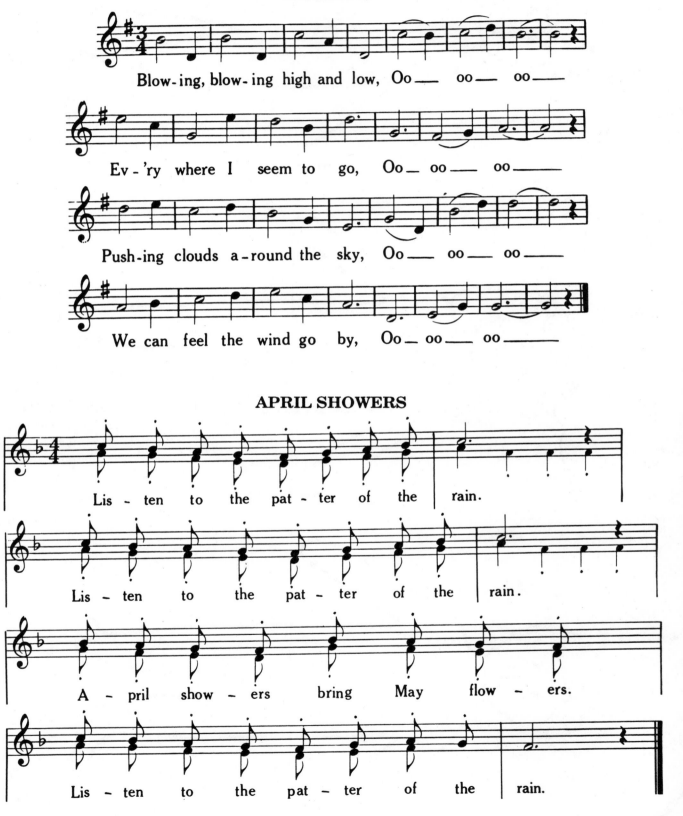

Blow-ing, blow-ing high and low, Oo__ oo__ oo__

Ev-'ry where I seem to go, Oo__ oo__ oo__

Push-ing clouds a-round the sky, Oo__ oo__ oo__

We can feel the wind go by, Oo__ oo__ oo__

APRIL SHOWERS

Lis - ten to the pat - ter of the rain.

Lis - ten to the pat - ter of the rain.

A - pril show - ers bring May flow - ers.

Lis - ten to the pat - ter of the rain.

WEATHER MUSIC ACTIVITIES

TAMBOURINE

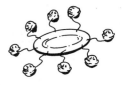

What you need: Styrofoam paper plates
Yarn
Markers
Bells
Stapler

What you do: Pre-cut yarn into six inch strings. Have the children use markers to decorate two plates. Use a paper punch to make six holes around the edge of the plates. Give each child a bell for each hole punched. Have the children thread the yarn through the bells and holes.

EENCY, WEENCY SPIDER

The eency, weency spider crawled up the waterspout.
Down came the rain and washed the spider out.
Out came the sun and dried up all the rain.
And the eency, weency spider crawled up the spout again.
(Use as a flannel board song.
The patterns are included.)

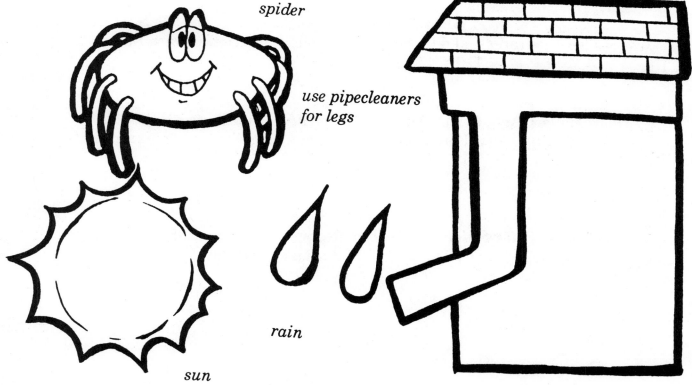

spider

use pipecleaners for legs

waterspout

rain

sun

SUGGESTED READING LIST

Davidson, Amanda. ***Teddy Goes Outside.*** Holt, Rinehart & Winston.
   Copyright © 1985. *Summary:* Teddy goes outside and participates in
   different activities in various kinds of weather.

Ets, Marie Hall. ***Gilberto and the Wind.*** Viking. Copyright © 1963.
   Summary: A young boy finds in the wind a playmate of many moods: one
   that can sail boats, fly kites, blow dirt and turn umbrellas inside out.

Hutchins, Pat. ***The Wind Blew.*** Macmillian Publishing. Copyright © 1974.
   Summary: A rhymed tale describing the antics of a capricious wind.

Kalan, Robert. ***Rain.*** Greenwillow Books. Copyright © 1978. *Summary:*
   Illustrations describe a rainstorm.

Rockwell, Anne. ***In The Rain.*** Crowell Books. Copyright © 1986. *Summary:*
   Color illustrations and text describe a child's experiences with rain.

Scheweninger, Ann. ***On My Way To Grandpa's.*** Dial Press. Copyright
   © 1987. *Summary:* Emily's trip to grandpa's house becomes a nature walk
   in the rain.

Spier, Peter. ***Peter Spier's Rain.*** Doubleday. Copyright © 1982. *Summary:*
   Two children play in their backyard during a rainy day.

ST. PATRICK'S DAY

CONTENTS

St. Patrick's Day Art Activities

RAINBOW FINGER PAINT

Have each of the children dip their fingers into finger paint. Each finger should be dipped into a different color. The children move their fingers across a piece of finger paint paper. This easy masterpiece will look like a rainbow. When the painting is dry, the children may wish to draw a pot of gold or something else that they would like to find at the end of their rainbow.

When the children have finished painting their rainbows, give the children time to experiment with the feel of the finger paint. Encourage them to use their fingers, palms, knuckles, etc.

Mount the children's creations on a larger piece of colored construction paper.

SHAMROCK STENCILS

The teacher will need to pre-cut cardboard shamrock shapes. *(Older children may wish to cut the shapes themselves.)* The children place the shamrock shape under a white piece of paper. Holding a crayon sideways, color over the paper until the shamrock appears. This is an easy project that is always successful. For a very young child coloring over a stencil is almost like magic!

POT OF GOLD

Have the children make a pot from black construction paper. The pot can be glued or pasted onto another sheet of colored construction paper. The children can fill their pots by gluing a yellow cereal on the top of the pot. Kix, Lucky Charms and Sugar Pops are some cereals that would provide very good "gold" for the children's "Pots-Of-Gold."

SHAMROCK

St. Patrick's Day Learning Games

WHAT IS ST. PATRICK'S DAY

This is a holiday in March that celebrates the myth of St. Patrick in Ireland. We celebrate this day on March 17th. Tell the children the myth of St. Patrick chasing the snakes out of Ireland to bring good luck to the people there. Explain Ireland's legend of the little people and the good luck that follows them. Their pot of gold is found at the end of the rainbow, if anyone can get there before the rainbow fades.

Ask the children to wear green to school for St. Patrick's Day. Locate some Irish music *(most libraries will help you to find Irish music that may be checked out.)* Teach the children how to dance the Irish Jig on St. Patrick's Day.

THE COLOR GREEN

St. Patrick's Day is a wonderful holiday for creating lots of "green" experiences. Besides wearing green to school and making green shamrocks, have the children make and play with green play dough, make green jello, and a very exciting treat GREEN MILKSHAKES. Using a blender, have the children make vanilla milk shakes. Add a little green food coloring and peppermint extract. Another way to create green milk shakes is to simply use peppermint bon bon ice cream. The children will love drinking these green milkshakes!

LEPRECHAUNS ARE LITTLE

The teacher will need to prepare picture cards. The picture cards should have two items on each card: one big item and one little item. For example, one big chair and one little chair. The next card could have a big bike and a little bike.

Explain to the children that Leprecauns are little. The children should look at the cards and decide which item would best be suited for a Leprechaun.

VARIATION FOR OLDER CHILDREN: Give each child a 3" x 5" index card. Have the children illustrate a picture of a Leprechaun's home. The small index card will force the children to draw a small picture, illustrating the fact that Leprechaun's are little and would have little things.

Reproducible Art Activity Pattern.
Enlarge pattern on 12 x 18 paper.
Color green.

Cut out

St. Patrick's Day Games

THE HIDING LEPRECHAUN

This game is very similar to "Hide and Seek." The difference is that only one person hides. The child who hides is the "Leprechaun." While the classroom of children close their eyes, the Leprechaun runs away and hides with his/her pot of gold. *(The teacher will need to prepare a construction paper pot of gold.)*

Once the Leprechaun is hidden, the other children begin searching. The child who finds the Leprechaun gets to take the Leprechaun's pot of gold and will be the next child to hide.

If you have a large class, this game will be more effective if you divide the children into groups of 5 to 10 children. Each group must only look for the child who is the Leprechaun for their group. The rest of the game is played the same.

FIND THE POT OF GOLD

The teacher should make a picture of a rainbow. Once your rainbow is prepared, cut it into puzzle pieces. Cover the rainbow puzzle pieces with clear contact paper or laminate them for durability *(and so you can save them for years to come!)*

After you have explained Leprechauns, rainbows and the pot of gold, tell the children that they are going on a gold hunt. Since the pot of gold is found at the end of the rainbow, they must first find all the pieces of the rainbow.

The teacher hides all the rainbow pieces. The children search for the pieces and as they find them they put the rainbow together. The child who locates the last piece of the rainbow is the one who is given the pot of gold. Repeat this game many times, so other children have the opportunity of being given the pot of gold.

A SPECIAL NOTE ABOUT THE PUZZLE PIECES: Depending on the age group that you teach will determine how many puzzle pieces you decide to cut from the rainbow. Preschoolers will probably only need to have 6 to 9 puzzle pieces, while second graders will really enjoy searching for and making a large rainbow of many pieces. You will have to decide how many puzzle pieces your classroom of children will be able to successfully complete.

What will you find at the end of the rainbow?

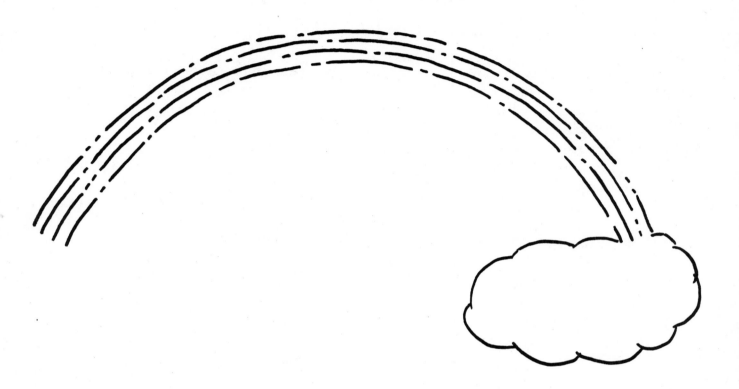

Name _____

MYRTLE, THE TURTLE,
MEETS A LEPRECHAUN

Myrtle, the turtle, was creeping along the road minding her own business and enjoying the smooth, soft feel of spring. Suddenly she saw a quick movement among a group of yellow daisies on the roadside.

"Who's that?" she asked, in a slow way. "Who's there?"

"Nobody here but us daisies," said a small voice.

Murtle smiled her slow smile. "Come on out," she said. "I won't hurt you, I promise."

A very small green man, with a green pointed hat, a bunch of whiskers on his chin and a crooked walking cane in his hand, pushed his way through the daisies. "Why hi there, Mr. Leprechaun," said Myrtle.

"Sure and you know who I am now?" asked the little green man.

"Of course," said Myrtle. "Everybody knows a Leprechaun when they see one! But what are you doing so far from home?"

"I decided to be taking a little trip and here I am," said the Leprechaun. "Now I suppose you'll be wanting me pot o' gold."

"No thank you," said Myrtle. "I most surely would not."

"Well," said the Leprechaun, sighing with relief. "Now, I'll just be givn' you your wish, then."

"I don't wish for anything, thank you," said Myrtle.

"Sure now," said the Leprechaun, "there must be something special that you're wanting."

"Well, yes," said Myrtle slowly, "I would like some pink ribbons for Ruthie Rabbit's birthday present."

"Whoosh!" complained the Leprechaun. "You've got to be wishing for your ownself now, according to proper form."

"Then I haven't any wishes," said Myrtle.

"You have to have," said the Leprechaun. "It's one of the rules of the Leprechauns. If ya don't take the gold, you get yourself a wish. It's a rule now, I'm telling ya!"

The Leprechaun tugged at his little beard. Then he snapped his fingers. "I know," he shouted, "Wouldn't it be grand to be the only turtle in the world with wings? And think how fast you could get around with wings."

Myrtle thought. After a long while she said, "Silver wings?" The Leprechaun nodded.

"All right, I'll take them," said Myrtle.

Myrtle closed her eyes and said, "I wish I had a lovely pair of silver wings," before her words were finished, there on her back was a pair of lovely silver wings.

"Go on," urged the Leprechaun. "Try your wings."

Myrtle spread her wings, and the first thing she knew, there she was flying high above the daisies and over the Leprechaun. She looked down. Myrtle felt dizzy. Then she heard a familiar voice.

"Why, Myrtle, think of seeing you up here!" And there was Robin Redbreast flying next to her.

"Yes," said Myrtle. "Just think of it."

"I'm here for the summer," said Robin. "And I must say I'm surprised to see you. I never saw a turtle fly."

"I think I'm surprised myself," said Myrtle. "And I do wish these wings wouldn't fly so fast."

"Try moving them more slowly," said Robin.

Myrtle tried. "I'm still going faster than I really want to," she said.

"I don't think you're so happy flying," said Robin.

"I know I'm not - how do I land?" exclaimed Myrtle.

Robin showed her how to use the wings for landing. Then he flew on. Myrtle came down with a dull thud. She looked all around. She was back where she had started. There was a little movement among the daisies.

"Mr. Leprechaun," said Myrtle, "Come out at once, please."

The little green man slowly pushed his way through the daisies. "Have a nice flight?" he asked.

"NO!" replied Myrtle, "I didn't!"

"Oh, dear now," said the Leprechaun. "You're suppose to be happy when your wish is granted. Whatever shall I do now?"

"Look," said Myrtle. "You gave me a wish, so you obeyed the rules. If you give me another wish, you'll be obeying the rules twice."

"Sure and you're right," said the little green man. "Close your eyes and be making it then."

Myrtle closed her eyes. "I wish I didn't have a pair of silver wings," she said, and suddenly she didn't! "I hope you're not offended," she replied.

"It's alright," said the Leprechaun. "And good luck to ye, Myrtle. 'Tis not many I meet who are to be satisfied with things as they be."

Myrtle glanced at her back just to make sure the wings were gone. When she turned around again the Leprechaun had disappeared. But there on the road where he had been standing was something pink and shiny. Myrtle crept up to it. There was a fancy pink ribbon with a lovely card reading, "Happy Birthday to Ruthie, from Myrtle, the Turtle." Myrtle smiled happily. "Well now," she said to herself. "Wasn't that a kind thing for him to do? He was certianly a nice fellow, wasn't he?"

(Flannel board patterns are found on pages 24 & 25.)

From Story Telling with the Flannel Board, Book Two. By Paul S. Anderson
Copyright © T.S. Denison & Co., Inc.

STORY PATTERNS

Patterns for the story, "Myrtle, the Turtle, Meets a Leprechaun,"
found on pages 22 - 23.

Myrtle, the Turtle

Pink Ribbon

Mr. Leprechaun

STORY PATTERNS

Patterns for the story, "Myrtle, the Turtle, Meets a Leprechaun," found on pages 22 - 23.

Silver Wings

Robin Redbreast

RHYMES/POETRY/MUSIC

LEPRECHUAN

Five tiny Leprechauns on St. Patrick's Day,
The first one said, "Let's have fun while we may."
The second one said, "Let's make a wish."
The third one said, "Let's catch a fish."
The fourth one said, "I want to laugh and play."
The fifth one said, "We better run away."
(Make finger puppets to dramatize the rhyme.
The pattern has been included. This rhyme can
help to develop ordinal number counting skills.)

TALL AND SMALL

Here is a giant who is tall, tall, tall;
    (children stand up tall)
Here is a leprechaun who is small, small, small;
    (children slowly sink to the floor)
The leprechaun who is small will try, try, try;
    (children slowly rise)
To reach the giant who is high, high, high.
    (children stand tall and reach high)

SHAMROCKS, SHAMROCKS

Shamrocks, shamrocks, on Ireland's hills,
Greenest of green, over rocks and hills.
Good Luck they do bring for one and for all.
On St. Patrick's Day we can see them all.

THE LEPRECHAUN

There's a lit-tle old man, with a green suit on. Watch out! He'll trick you if he can, 'cause he's a lep-re-chaun!

St. Patrick's Day Bulletin Board

LEPRECHAUN LAND

Cover the bulletin board with white paper. Let the children paint a large rainbow on the white paper. When the rainbow is dry, the children can make construction paper leprechauns and colored tissue paper flowers. Let the children arrange their leprechauns all over the rainbow. Some of the leprechauns can hide under the rainbow; some can be sliding down the rainbow, etc. Let the children be creative when then are working on this bulletin board.

When finished, this bulletin board is beautiful!

SUGGESTED READING LIST

Asch, Frank. *Skyfire.* Prentice-Hall. Copyright © 1984. *Summary:* When he sees a rainbow for the first time, Bear thinks that the sky is on fire and he is determined to put out the skyfire.

Bunting, Eve. *St. Patrick's Day in the Morning.* Houghton/Mifflin/Clarion Books. Copyright © 1980. *Summary:* Jamie seeks a way to prove he is not too young to march in the St. Patrick's Day parade.

Freeman, Don. *Rainbow Of My Own.* Viking. Copyright © 1966. *Summary:* A small boy imagines what it would be like to have his own rainbow to play with.

Janice. *Little Bear Marches in the St. Patrick's Day Parade.* Lothrop. Copyright © 1967.

Schertle, Alice. *Jeremy Bean's St. Patrick's Day.* Lothrop, Lee & Shepard Books. Copyright © 1987. *Summary:* Shy Jeremy Bean, much to his humiliation forgets to wear green to school.

Weston, Martha. *Peony's Rainbow.* Lothrop, Lee & Shepard Books. Copyright © 1981. *Summary:* Relates the adventures of Peony Pig who wanted a rainbow of her very own and what she did when she got one.

THE FARM AND FARM ANIMALS

CONTENTS

FARM ANIMAL ART ACTIVITIES

CLOTHESPIN ANIMALS

Provide each child with a cardboard cut-out of a farm animal. *(Older children will perfer to make their own cut-outs)* The cut-out of the animal should not have any legs. The children either color or paint the animal and then place clothespins on the base of the animal for legs. These animals will stand up.

To make this an extra special activity, turn a table top into a farm scene. Using boxes you can create a barn, fences and pens. Use foil to represent a pond. Display all your clothespin animals on the table top farm scene.

PAPER BAG PIG

You will need: paper lunch bags; pink and black construction paper; markers; glue.

Pre-cut the pieces for the pig for those children who are unable to cut the pieces by themselves. Have the children glue the pieces of the pig onto the paper bag. When the children have finished their paper bag pig puppet, you can have the children sing, "Old McDonald had a pig," or make up a story or song with the class.

The children will also enjoy making paper bag puppets of all the different farm animals.

PIGGY BANK

You will need: 64 oz. (1/2 gal.) Clorox or Hilex bottle, 1 for each child; 1" diameter corks, cut in half, 4 halves for each child; Brown construction paper; pink construction paper; pink pipe cleaners, 1 for each child; glue; markers.

What you do: 1) Clean bottles before class, remove lables.

2) Cut quarter size slot in top (handle side).

3) Cut pink circle to cover top of screw cap.

4) Cut brown irregular shapes for spots on body; glue in place.

5) Use magic markers to draw eyes under handle location.

6) Poke small hole in flat end for tail; then wrap pipe cleaner around a pencil to form coil and insert at least 1" into hole.

7) Attach (glue) corks to bottom for feet.

8) Glue pink ears in place.

FARM ANIMAL ART ACTIVITIES

CHUBBY CHICKENS

Each child will need a lunch bag. Stuff the bag with crumbled newspaper. Tie a string around the top of the bag to keep the stuffing inside. Make a chicken head from construction paper and staple the head onto the top of the lunch bag. Wings and other decorations can be painted on the bag.

Older children will enjoy trying to make other types of animals with the stuffed lunch bags.

ROCK DUCKS

Ask each of the children to bring two small rocks to school. One rock must be larger than the other *(look at the illustration next to this activity)*. The rocks should be as smooth as possible.

Using household cement, glue the smaller rock on the top of the larger rock. The smaller rock will be the duck's head and should also be placed near the edge on the top of the larger rock.

Once the cement is dry, the children may paint their rocks yellow. When the yellow paint is dry, facial features and the outline of wings can be added.

FARM ANIMAL MASKS

Strong paper plates can make beautiful masks. Let the children make animal masks with a variety of materials; paint, crayons, markers, glue, scrap fabric, etc. Styrofoam cups can make interesting noses and ears.

Cut eye holes and attach tongue depressors as handles. These masks are meant to be held in front of the face. The children will not only enjoy making these masks, but will have hours of enjoyment using them in creative play and story telling.

Farm Animal Crossword Puzzle

WORD BANK

Directions: Fill in the crossword puzzle with the words below.

chicken	pig	cow	ducks
sheep	horse	goat	cat

FARM ANIMAL LANGUAGE ACTIVITIES

MY FARM ANIMAL BOOK

The teacher should prepare pictures of various farm animals that can be reproduced for each child in the class. Each day of the farm unit introduce a new farm animal and give the child a picture of that animal. The children may wish to color the animal and add other objects to the picture, such as the animal's living shelter.

Instead of drawing the pictures of the animals for the children, the children may wish to draw their own pictures. At the end of the unit the children will have a nice collection of all the animals that they have learned about. Bind each child's collection of pictures into book form. The children may also wish to dictate sentences about each animal. These sentences can be written by the teacher under the picture. Older children will enjoy writing their own sentences.

BO-PEEP FIND YOUR SHEEP

The teacher will need to prepare cut-outs of Bo-Peep and numbered sheep. The child chosen to play the role of Bo-Peep stands infront of the class holding the Bo-Peep cut-out. The children sit in a circle, with numbered sheep.

While the class recites the rhyme, she pretends to be searching for her lost sheep. She calls them in sequence. The children with the numbered sheep respond as their numerals are called by showing their numerals to the class and then lining up behind Bo-Peep until all the sheep are found.

This game can be made more difficult as more numerals are added, or as they are called out of sequence.

SORT ANIMAL CRACKERS

Animal crackers can provide excellent sorting and matching experiences for children. (And the best part is once you have finished the task, one gets to eat the assignment!)

FARM ANIMAL GAMES

LITTLE BOY BLUE

Let the children pretend to be Little Boy Blue. Have them lie on the floor (or mats) and pretend to be sleeping while the teacher reads this rhyme. To add another opportunity for participation, have some of the children pretend they are sheep while others pretend to be cows. Have them sneak away from Boy Blue as he falls asleep, going to areas designated as the "meadow" and the "corn field."

Provide the children with an outline of a sheep on a piece of construction paper. Have the children glue cotton onto the sheep.

Little Boy Blue,	Where is the boy	Will you wake him?
Come Blow your horn!	Who looks after the sheep?	No, not I!
The sheeps in the meadow,	He's under the haystack,	For if I do,
The cows in the corn.	Fast asleep!	He's sure to cry!

ANIMAL GUESS

Cut pictures of animals (two of each animal) out of magazines or coloring books. Pin one picture on each child's back. All the children should move around the room behaving like the picture of the animal on their back. The object is for the children to locate their matching animal.

ANIMAL SOUNDS

Children are fascinated by tape recorders. As a group project, let each of the children individually record a farm animal sound in the tape recorder. Once the tape is completed, play the sounds back for the children and have the children guess what farm animal makes that sound and guess who the child was that made that particular sound.

MY FARM SCENE

Name _____

This is a farm. But where are the animals?
Can you draw pictures of some of the animals that
should live on this farm?

FARM MUSIC ACTIVITIES

THE FARMER IN THE DELL

All children enjoy the song and the game of *"The Farmer in the Dell."* For those of you who may have forgotten the sequence of the song, it goes like this: The farmer takes a wife; the wife takes a child; the child takes a nurse; the nurse takes a dog; the dog takes a cat; the cat takes a rat; the rat takes some cheese; and the cheese is left standing alone.

WHAT CAN YOU DO ON THE FARM?
(Sing to the tune of - "Oh, Be Careful Little Hands What You Do?)

Oh, what can you do at the farm?
Oh, what can you do at the farm?
Say, "Moo" to the cow.
He will show you how.
That's what you can do at the farm!

Oh, what can you do at the farm?
Oh, what can you do at the farm?
Watch out for the goat.
For he might eat your coat!
That's what you can do at the farm.

Oh, what can you do at the farm?
Oh, what can you do at the farm?
Plant a few seeds.
And help pull up the weeds.
That's what you can do at the farm.

Oh, what can you do at the farm?
Oh, what can you do at the farm?
Gather eggs each day.
And feed horses hay.
That's what you can do at the farm.

MY PET DUCK

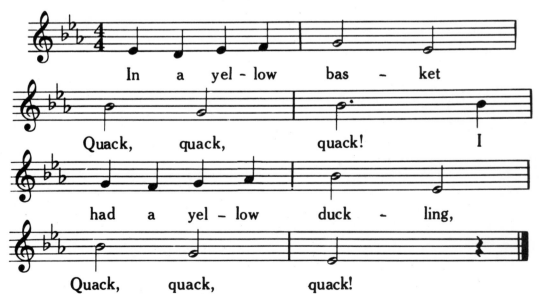

FARM ANIMAL STORY

FIVE LITTLE MICE

Five little mice went out to play,
Over the field and far away.
Mother mouse said, "Squeak, squeak, squeak."
Four little mice came out to peek.

Four little mice went out to play.
Over the field and far away.
Mother mouse said, "Squeak, squeak, squeak."
Three little mice came out to peek.

Three little mice went out to play.
Over the field and far away.
Mother mouse said, "Squeak, squeak, squeak."
Two little mice came out to peek.

Two little mice came out to play.
Over the field and far away.
Mother mouse said, "Squeak, squeak, squeak."
One little mouse came out to peek.

One little mouse came out to play.
Over the field and far away.
Mother mouse said, "Squeak, squeak, squeak."
No little mice came out to peek.

No little mice went out to play.
Over the field and far away.
FATHER MOUSE said, "SQUEAK, SQUEAK, SQUEAK."
Five little mice came out to peek.

Using the patterns make five little mice and one mother mouse. Attach paper clips to mice. Set up a shallow cardboard box straddling two tables, allowing enough room around the box for the children to be able to reach under it. Teach the children the rhyme, Five Little Mice. Have the children act out the rhyme, using magnets under the box to make the mice move.

Bend paper clips like this.

Mother Mouse

Make five little mice.

FARM ANIMAL RHYMES/POETRY

RICKY ROOSTER
Ricky Rooster is round and red,
And every morning he makes this sound -
      Er-er-er-er-errrrr!
No matter if the day is dark,
He never fails to let it start
      With Er-er-er-er-errrrr!
Now Ricky Rooster is so wise,
He knows just when the sun should rise -
      Er-er-er-er-errrrr!
I need not get up with a clock -
Ricky Rooster's my tick-tock!

MOO-MOO COW
Mirandy is my moo-moo cow,
    Who lives out at the farm.
She moos out in the pasture;
    She moos down in the barn!
She moos and moos at everything -
    The mailman and the moon;
She even moos at being milked -
    What's more - she moos off tune!
My father said, "We'll change her name -
    She's not Mirandy now;
If all she wants to do is moo -
    We'll call her "Moo-Moo Cow!"

ANIMALS ON THE FARM
One little mouse, squeaky, squeak.
Two little kittens, peekety - peek.
Three little puppies, bow-wow-wow.
Four little roosters, cock-a-doodle-doo.
Five old hens, clack, clack, clack.
Six fat ducks, quack, quack, quack.
(Children are choosen to play the roles
of one mouse, two kittens, etc. Each
group may make the animal sounds.
Ask, "How would a mouse move? a duck?
a rooster?)
From Rhymes for Learning Times.
By Louise Binder Scott
Copyright © T.S. Denison & Co., Inc.

THE LITTLE RED HEN

One day, about noon-time, in the back of the farmyard, some of the animals realized they were hungry and getting hungrier.

"I'm hungry," the dog gruffed. "And there are no bones to chew on."

"I'm hungry, too," the cat mewed. "And there's no saucer of milk to drink."

"I'm hungry, too," the duck quacked. "And there are no fresh bugs or grass in the pond to eat."

"I'm a little hungry," said the Little Red Hen, who was pecking and picking at grains and seeds in the farmyard. "It would be nice to have a loaf of bread made out of wheat." All the other animals looked up. Next to the farmyard there was a golden field of wheat, stretching as far as their eyes could see.

"Let's do it," the dog gruffed. "A big fresh loaf of bread!"

"Let's do it," the cat mewed. "A big warm fresh loaf of bread!"

"Let's do it," the duck quacked. "A big warm crispy fresh loaf of bread!"

"All right," said the Little Red Hen. "But we must work together. First of all, someone has to go out in the field and gather the wheat."

"I would, but I'm too tired," the dog gruffed, yawning a big yawn.

"I would, but I'm too small," the cat mewed, trying to look smaller.

"I would, but I'm too busy," the duck quacked, looking around for something to do.

"Oh, all right," said the Little Red Hen. "I'll do it."

And she did. She stepped out in the field and gathered the wheat. It was hard getting all the grains of wheat down from the tall stalks around her, but she did it. She gathered enough to make a big warm crispy fresh loaf of bread. Then she came back to the farmyard.

"Now we need to grind the wheat in the mill," said the Little Red Hen.

"I would, but I'm still too tired," the dog gruffed, yawning a big yawn.

"I would, but I'm still too small," the cat mewed, trying to look smaller.

"I would, but I'm still too busy," the duck quacked, looking around for something to do.

"Oh, all right," said the Little Red Hen. "I'll do it."

And she did. She went inside the house and poured the wheat into a mill and turned the wheel. It was hard turning the wheel to get all that wheat ground into flour, but she did it. She ground enough flour to make a big warm crispy fresh load of bread. Then she came back into the farmyard.

"Now we need to make the flour into dough in the kitchen," said the Little Red Hen.

"I would, but I'm very tired," the dog gruffed, yawning a big yawn.

"I would, but I'm very small," the cat mewed, trying to look smaller.

"I would, but I'm very busy," the duck quacked, looking around for something to do.

"Oh, all right," said the Little Red Hen. "I'll do it."

And she did. She mixed the flour and added the water and added the yeast and kneaded the dough. It was hard to knead all that sticky dough, but she did it. She kneaded enough dough to make a big warm crispy freash loaf of bread. The she came back to the farmyard.

"Now we need to bake the dough," said the Little Red Hen.

"I would, but I'm terribly tired," the dog gruffed, yawning a big yawn.

"I would, but I'm terribly small," the cat mewed, trying to look smaller.

"I would, but I'm terribly busy," the duck quacked, looking around for something to do.

"Oh, all right," said the Little Red Hen. "I'll do it."

And she did. She put the loaf of dough into the hot oven. It was hard to shut the big oven door, but she did it. She watched it carefully until it baked to a beautiful golden brown. The smell of the fresh bread drifted out to the farmyard where the other animals were and they all came running in the door.

"Time to eat the big fresh bread," the dog gruffed, not yawning anymore.

"Time to eat the big fresh bread," mewed the cat, not trying to look small anymore.

"Time to eat the big fresh bread," the duck quacked, not trying to look busy anymore.

"Oh, no!" said the Little Red Hen. "I gathered the wheat from the field, and I ground the flour on the mill. I kneaded the dough in the kitchen and I baked the loaf in the oven. Now I am going to eat it!"

And she did! She took it out in the farmyard and pecked and picked at the big warm crispy fresh loaf of golden brown bread until it was all crumbs and gone. Then she went into the chicken house and took a nap.

The dog and the cat and the duck just stood in the farmyard and looked at each other, as hungry as they were before, and probably a little bit hungrier.

(Use the patterns found on pages 41 & 42 to turn "The Little Red Hen" into a flannel board story.)

STORY PATTERNS

Patterns for the story "The Little Red Hen," found on pages 39 - 40.

STORY PATTERNS

Patterns for the story "The Little Red Hen," found on pages 39 - 40.

THE TWO CHICKS

Once there were two baby chicks that wanted to see the world. One was as black as coal. One was as white as chalk.

"Cheep, cheep," said the black chick. "Let us see the world."

"Chirp, chirp," said the white chick. "Let us see the world."

So they set out on their way. Soon they met Gray squirrel. "Chatter, chatter," said Grey Squirrel. "Where are you going, chicks."

"Cheep," said the black one, "to see the world."

"Chirp," said the white one, "to see the world."

The baby chicks went on their way. Soon they met old Dobbin, the horse. He was eating hay. "Chomp, chomp," where are you going, chicks?" he asked.

"Cheep," said the black one, "to see the world."

"Chirp," said the white one, "to see the world."

But Dobbin, the horse, went on eating, "chomp, chomp," and smiled a bit at the silly chicks.

The two chicks were tired. They thought they had traveled so far that they must nearly be at the end of the earth.

"Oh, cheep, we are lost," cried the black one.

"Oh, chirp, we are lost," cried the white one.

But a robin heard them. "Cheer-up, cheer-up," he cried and gave them a cherry to eat. "You'll find your way home," he said, "cheer-up, cheer-up," and he laughed.

"We are so far from home. Why do they laugh?" asked the chicks. Then they went around a bush and what do you think they saw? Their own chicken coop, with Mother Chicken calling them. They rushed up to her.

"Oh, Mother, cheep, cheep, we have been around the world," said the black one.

"Oh, Mother, chirp, chirp, we have been around the world," said the white one. Mother Chicken laughed.

"Why, you haven't been out of the farmyard," she said. The chicks looked around. And sure enough they hadn't!

From Story Telling with the Flannel Board, Book One By Paul S. Anderson.
Copyright © T.S. Denison & Co., Inc.

Story Patterns

Patterns for the story, "The Two Chicks," found on page 43.

Gray Squirrel

Make one white
and one black.

Mother Hen

Robin

Farm Animal
Multi-Purpose Patterns

FARM ANIMAL
MULTI-PURPOSE PATTERNS

Suggested Reading List

Brandenberg, Franz. *Cock-A-Doodle-Doo.* Greenwillow Books. Copyright ©
1986. *Summary:* The animal and human inhabitants of a farm, quack,
neigh, say "Shoo! Shoo!" and otherwise communicate in their own fashion.

Brown, Margaret Wise. *Big Red Barn.* Harper & Row, Copyright © 1989.
Summary: Rhymed text and illustrations introduce the many different
animals that live in the Big Red Barn.

Carle, Eric. *The Very Busy Spider.* Philomel Books. Copyright © 1984.
Summary: The farm animals try to divert a busy little spider from
spinning her web, but she persists and produces a thing of both beauty
and usefulness.

Forrester, Victoria. *The Magnificent Moo.* Atheneum Books. Copyright
© 1983. *Summary:* When a cow trades her moo for a cat's meow because
she thinks it too loud, the moo gets traded in turn to several other
animals until it finally returns to a more satisfied cow.

Gammel, Steven. *Once Upon McDonald's Farm.* Four Winds Press.
Copyright © 1981. *Summary:* McDonald tries farming with exotic farm
circus animals, but has better luck with his neighbor's cow, horse and
chicken.

Galdone, Paul. *The Cat Goes Fiddle-i-Fee.* Clarion Books. Copyright
© 1985. *Summary:* An old English rhyme names all the animals a boy
feeds on his daily rounds.

Griffth, Helen. *Grandaddy's Place.* Greenwillow Books. Copyright © 1987.
Summary: At first Janetta does not like her Grandaddy, his farm, or his
animals - but they like her and as she gets used to them, she likes them
too.

Provensen, Alice. *A Horse and a Hound, A Goat and a Gander.*
Atheneum. Copyright © 1979. *Summary:* Four farm animals each with a
distinct and highly idiosyncratic personality liven up the days at Maple
Hill Farm.

SPRINGTIME

—— CONTENTS ——

VINYL FLOWERS

Let the children cut flowers (petals, leaves, etc.) and baskets from vinyl wallpaper. *(Sample wall paper books can be obtained from wallpaper stores and decorator shops.)* The pieces of the flowers can be glued onto construction paper for a finished product or the pieces can be saved and used again and again for creating different types of flower arrangements.

SUNFLOWER

Have the children make a round yellow sunflower from construction paper. Gluing "REAL" sunflower seeds in the middle is a fun extra touch. Tape the sunflower to a plastic drinking straw. Arrange all the flowers in a vase. The flowers will stay in a vase well if styrofoam is place in the bottom of the vase and the straw stems are pushed into the styrofoam. Your flower arrangement will be most impressive!

TISSUE PAPER FLOWERS

Working with glue and tissue paper is always a lot of fun. Let the children enjoy gluing a wide variety of colored tissue paper onto a sheet of white paper. When the glue is dry, let the children cut out the shape of flowers from the tissue paper design. The flower shapes can be glued onto another sheet of paper. Add stems and leaves with markers or crayons.

My Flower Garden

Draw a flower on each of the stems. Color each flower a different color.

Name _____

SPRINGTIME LEARNING GAMES

WHAT IS GOOD TO EAT?

Children are usually aware of the fact that farms have a variety of animals, but young children are often surprised at the number of foods that are grown on a farm. This is the time of year that farmers and other people begin their planting. Spend some time with your children discussing all the different types of foods that are grown on a farm.

Set up a display of empty cereal boxes, egg cartons, milk cartons, cans and boxes of other foods. As an added surprise, include real fruits and vegetables. Give the children an opportunity to examine all the materials. Plan a meal using the materials you have on display. What foods would make an appropriate meal? Which foods are grown? Where are the foods grown? What are some of the children's favorite foods?

PLANT A GARDEN

For those of you who are lucky enough to teach in a year round program, this activity is a must! Find some space outside where you can actually till up a small vegetable garden. Give the children the opportunity to hoe the soil and enjoy the "dirt" before you plant the seeds. Plant a variety of vegetables. The children will delight in watching the growth of the plants. Come harvest time, the children will feel so accomplished to finally get to eat some of the wonderful things that they helped to plant and care for all summer.

If you cannot find any space outside, it is possible to plant vegetables in large containers in the classroom.

POP-UP FLOWERS

Each child will make a flower from construction paper. Glue the flower onto the top of a tongue depressor. The tongue depressor can be poked through the bottom of a styrofoam cup.

When you are discussing springtime and planting, this activity can work well to help visualize how a plant grows. Pull the flower into the cup so it cannot be seen. Tell the children how one plants a seed *(pantomiming planting the seed in the cup)*. Then, after you have pantomined planting the seed, watering the seed, and providing the seed with sunlight, slowly push the tongue depressor up to demonstrate the flower growing. The children can tell their parents about how seeds grow when they bring their pop-up flowers home.

Draw some spring flowers. Name _____

Color The Flower

Name _____

SPRINGTIME RHYMES/POETRY

WHEN SPRING CAME

A turtle and a frog one day
Were sitting in the sun;
And happy as they could be were they
For spring was time for fun.

A mother robin heard them chat,
And frowned upon the two.
She wondered why they had to say.
She had so much to do.

With grass and string she made a nest -
So beautiful, so round.
She smoothed it with her feathered
    breast
And mud that she had found.

And when her work was done, she laid
Some eggs of lovely blue.
And on them, patiently she stayed
To warm them through and through.

One day the baby birds were hatched
And feeding was begun,
So robin hunted wiggly worms
To feed them one by one.

The turtle found a place to swim,
The frog a lily pad,
But robin sat upon a limb
And sang, for she was glad.

TULIPS

Five little tulips bright and gay,
    (hold up fingers and thumb on one hand)
Let us water them each day.
    (make sprinkle motion with other hand)
Watch them open in the bright sunlight,
    (cup hand, then open)
Watch them when it is night.
    (close hand again)

FLOWERS

Flowers tall,
    (let tall fingers stand up)
Flowers small,
    (let little finger and thumb stand up)
Count them one by one,
Blowing with the breezes
In the springtime sun!
1, 2, 3, 4, 5.
    (touch each finger as you count)
From, *Rhymes for Fingers and Flannel Boards.*
By Louise Binder Scott and J.J. Thompson.
Copyright © T.S. Denison & Co., Inc.

SPRINGTIME BULLETIN BOARD

SPRINGTIME

This is a beautiful bulletin board! Cover the background of the bulletin board with light blue paper on the top to represent the sky and green paper on the bottom to represent grass. The teacher or several able student may cut several tree trunks to be placed on the background. Large green circular cut outs can be made for the leaves at the top of the tree.

The children can crumple and glue on pink tissue paper blossoms on the leaves of the trees. *(If you give the blossoms a small squirt of perfume, your bulletin board will actually smell like spring!)* Flowers, animals, and children playing can also be added to the background.

SPRINGTIME BULLETIN BOARD

THINK SPRING

If you live in a climate that has snow, you should finally be experiencing some warmer weather. Talk about the changing seasons. What types of activities can be done when the warmer weather arrives? Have the children cut-out pictures from magazines or draw their own pictures of springtime activities. Back the pictures in colored construction paper to "frame" the children's work. Add the caption, "THINK SPRING."

SPRINGTIME MUSIC ACTIVITIES

SPRINGTIME FLING

Play any rhythm record. The children should feel free to improvise by walking, dancing, or skipping to the record. Have the children choose partners, and teach them how to link arms and dance around in circles.

SPRING WILL SOON BE HERE

Spring will soon be hear,   We know it by the sign;   We can hear its whis – pers in the ma – ples and the pines.

SUGGESTED READING LIST

Alexander, Sue. *There's More, Much More.* Hartcourt Brace Jovanovich: Gulliver Books. Copyright © 1987. *Summary:* Squirrel and Sherri celebrate spring by collecting it in their May Baskets.

Forrester, Victoria. *The Touch Said Hello.* Atheneum. Copyright © 1982. *Summary:* The new leaves hidden inside an old oak tree impatiently await the coming of spring which will bring them and the tree back to life.

McNaughton, Colin. *Spring.* Dial Books for Young Readers. Copyright © 1984. *Summary:* Brief text and illustrations portray some of the activities and characteristics of spring.

Minarik, Else Holmelund. *It's Spring.* Greenwillow Books. Copyright © 1989. *Summary:* Pit and Pat celebrate the arrival of spring by jumping over each other and through the spring flowers.

Rockwell, Anne. *My Spring Robin.* Macmillian Publishing. Copyright © 1989. *Summary*: Before finding a robin she is searching for, a young girl discovers other interesting fauna and flora in the backyard.

Roth, Harold. *Spring Days.* Grosset and Dunlap. Copyright © 1986. *Summary:* Color photos and text describe children enjoying various springtime activities.

Rylant, Cynthia. *Henry and Mudge in Puddle Trouble.* Bradbury Press. Copyright © 1987. *Summary:* For Henry and his big dog Mudge, spring means playing in the puddles in the rain and watching the five new kittens next door.

Zolotow, Charlotte. *One Step, Two ...* Lothrop, Lee and Shepard Books. Copyright © 1981. *Summary:* While out for a walk on a spring morning a little girl shows her mother things grown-ups sometimes miss.

EASTER

AND

BUNNIES

━━━━━ CONTENTS ━━━━━

EASTER ACTIVITIES

GIANT EASTER EGGS

Each child in your class will need a blown-up balloon. Dip string into liquid starch. Wrap the starch string around the balloon. Hang the balloons until the starch is dry. Once the string is dry, pop the balloon. You will be left with a beautiful "lacey" egg-shaped ornament.

The children can use white glue and add glitter and sequins to their "giant eggs." Glitter should be added before the balloon is popped. Hang them from the ceiling.

EGGS-OUT-OF-A-BASKET MOBILE

You will need: Wire or straw basket; wire for hanging basket and shells; seven or more egg shells; food coloring, easter egg dye, and or paint; assorted fabric scraps; beads, lace, stickers, sequins, etc.

What you do: Empty the egg shells by carefully tapping small holes in both ends of the raw eggs and blowing out the contents. (Be sure to break the membrane around the yolk when making the holes in the shells.) The eggs can be used for cooking scrambled eggs, omelets, cakes, etc. with the children as chefs.

Dye the eggs and add beads, sequins, fabric, etc. to trim them. Glue string or thread to the top of each egg with white glue. Allow it to dry thoroughly before hanging. Attach to basket and suspend completed mobile from ceiling with string or wire.

REAL BUNNIES

In some parts of the country, during the Easter season, the Animal Humane Society will allow people to borrow a bunny for a few days. Call your local Animal Humane Society and check to see if you could borrow a bunny for your classroom. If this is not possible, bring in pictures and storybooks about rabbits. Discuss how they look, how they move and what they feel like.

Romper Rabbit

Directions: *Using a paint brush, brush white glue over the rabbit. Cover the rabbit in cotton.*

Easter Bunny Maze

EASTER BASKETS

Small milk cartons such as the children use daily make good baskets. Open, clean, dry and push up straight the four sides at the top of the carton. Trim away two of these side tops and curve the remaining two. Mix paint with a small amount of soap flakes (*not detergent*) and a little liquid paste or glitter glue, so that the paint will stick to the sides of the waxed carton. Colors such as purple will need two coats unless the tempera is very thick. When dry, attach a handle to the two curved top sides (*pipe cleaner will do*). Fill the basket with green Easter "grass." Put in a real colored egg to take home.

BUNNY BASKET

Cut a hole in a large cylinder container (*as an oatmeal box*). Tape top lid. Attach paper rabbit ears on one lid and paper feet on the other. Glue on cotton for a tail. Add construction paper eyes and pipe cleaner whiskers. Fill the bunny with artificial grass.

CARROT CAKE

You will need: 2 cups sifted flour, 1 cup sugar, 2 teaspoons baking soda, 1 teaspoon salt, 4 eggs, 1 cup salad oil, 2 cups shredded carrots, 2 teaspoons cinnamon, 2 teaspoons baking powder.

What you do: Sift together flour, sugar, cinnamon, baking soda, baking powder, and salt in a large bowl. Beat eggs slightly in another bowl. Add the eggs to the dry mixture and mix well. Add salad oil slowly. Stir in carrots and mix well. Turn into well-buttered cake pans. Bake at 350° degrees for 35 to 40 minutes.

Easter Games

DON'T BREAK THE EGG

This game is played the same as "Hot Potato," only substituting the potato for an egg. I would suggest using a L'eggs container, or an egg which has been emptied. Only the bravest of the the brave would use a real uncooked egg.

WHAT BUNNY DO YOU HEAR?

This game is always a favorite of young children.

Position several children at different parts of one section of the room. Have one child watch this positioning and then close his/her eyes or turn his/her back to the children. Have the positioned children speak or shout one at a time. The child turned around has to identify the name and position of the child who shouts. The child can identify by pointing *(still with eyes closed or turned around)* or by explaining which part of the room the shouting child is in.

This task can work as a game. Divide the children into two teams: one team working as the sounders and the other team as the identifiers.

THE BUNNY HOP

Remember when you were a child and danced the "Bunny Hop" in physical education class or in your classroom? Well, this song and dance is still a big hit with young children. Ask your librarian is she could locate a record which would have the "Bunny Hop" on it for you.

COLOR THE EGG

EASTER BULLETIN BOARD

THE EASTER EGG HUNT

   This is a fun and easy bulletin board for you and the children to create. Have each of the children draw, color or paint and cut out a large Easter egg. Pin the Easter eggs on the bulletin board. The teacher should draw a path that connects all of the eggs. This is the path that the bunny took when hiding all the eggs. The children may also wish to add flowers, bushes, rocks and trees to their "Easter Egg Hunt" scene.

Rabbit Puzzle

EASTER RHYMES/POETRY/MUSIC

LITTLE BROWN RABBIT

A little brown rabbit, *(make a fist)*
Popped out of the ground. *(use thumb to pop up)*
Wiggled his whiskers and *(wiggle fingers)*
Looked all around. *(look around)*
Another little brown rabbit, *(make another fist, use other thumb)*
Who lived in the grass. *(lay five fingers on the floor)*
Poked out his head to watch him pass. *(put hand above eyes, move thumb across)*
Then with a hop, hop, hop. *(make hopping motion with thumb)*
They would not stop. *(shake head "no")*
Two little rabbits hopped out of sight. *(make two thumbs hop behind your back)*
Right into the night!

HERE'S A BUNNY

Here is a bunny with ears so funny, *(extend index finger and middle finger of hand upward)*

And here is his hole in the ground. *(put other hand on hip)*
When he hears a noise *(clap hands loudly)*
He perks up his ears *(extend index finger and middle finger upward)*
And runs to his hole in the ground. *(put bunny in hole)*

HOPPER

The nose of a bunny
Is twitchy and funny. *(wrinkle nose several times)*
His furry ears flippety-flop. *(put hand on top of head and wiggle back and forth)*
His tail you can see
Is as small as can be *(put one hand behind back and wiggle it)*
But my, how his hind legs can HOP! *(hop around room)*

BUNNY

(Tune - Skip to My Lou)
Bunny, bunny hop all around.
Here and there, over the ground.

Are you looking for a treat?
Juicy carrots you can eat.

Bunny, bunny, how you hop!
Fast and slow and then you stop.

Fur so soft and ears so tall,
You're the finest pet of all.

THE EASTER BUNNIES

(tune - Mary had a Little Lamb)
The bunnies hop, hop down the trail,
Down the trail, down the trail.

The bunnies hop, hop down the trail,
Twitching their noses and wiggling
their tails.

They carry baskets with many treats,
Many treat, many treats.

They carry baskets with many treats,
For every boy and girl they meet.

FIVE LITTLE EASTER BUNNIES

Five little bunnies hopping all around.
The first bunny said, "I'm going to town."
The second bunny said, "I'll hide the eggs."
The third bunny said, "I will stretch my legs."

The fourth bunny said, "I'll eat a carrot."
The fifth bunny said, "I'll scare a parrot."
Five little bunnies so soft and furry.
Ran around the yard in such a hurry.

*(This is an excellent rhyme to be used on the flannel board.
Patterns have been included.)*

The Easter Bunny

SUGGESTED READING LISTS

Adams, Adrienne. *The Easter Egg Artists*. Scribner. Copyright © 1976.
Summary: The Abbotts, established Easter Egg Artists, but let their son
develop a style of his own when he shows interest in painting.

Armour, Richard. *The Adventures of Egbert the Easter Egg.* McGraw.
Copyright © 1965. *Summary:* Egbert, the Easter Egg isn't found during
the Easter egg hunt, and what's worse, he isn't even missed.

Friedrich, Pricilla. *The Easter Bunny that Overslept.* Lothrop, Lee and
Shepard Books. Copyright © 1983. *Summary:* Having slept past Easter,
the Easter Bunny tries to distribute his eggs on other holidays but no one
wants them. Finally on Christmas, Santa Claus gets him back on track.

Kroll, Steven. *The Big Bunny and the Easter Eggs.* Holiday House.
Copyright © 1982. *Summary:* Poor Wilbur, the Easter Bunny, gets so sick
that he almost misses his Easter deliveries.

Miller, Edna. *Mousekin's Easter Basket.* Prentice-Hall Books for Young
Readers. Copyright © 1986. *Summary:* After a harsh winter, Mousekin's
springtime search for food brings him in contact with brightly colored
eggs, a white rabbit and other symbols of Easter.

Stevenson, James. *The Great Big Especially Beautiful Easter Egg.*
Greenwillow Books. Copyright © 1983. *Summary:* At Easter a man tells
his two grandchildren how he searched many years ago for a special
Easter egg to give to his friend Charlotte.

Wolf, Winifred. *The Easter Bunny.* Dial Books for Young Readers.
Copyright © 1986. *Summary:* Contradicts doubts about the existence of
the Easter Bunny with stories that give evidence to the animals magical
place in Easter tradition.

SAFETY

CONTENTS

SAFETY RULES

Rule 1. **OBEY TRAFFIC SIGNS** - Learn what the colors of the traffic light mean. And remember to look both ways when you cross the street.

Rule 2. **PLAY SAFE** - Remember to share and take turns. Playing safe helps to prevent accidents.

Rule 3. **KNOW YOUR TELEPHONE NUMBER AND ADDRESS** - It is important to know your address and telephone number. If you were ever lost, you could tell a helping adult.

Rule 4. **KNOW THE EMERGENCY NUMBER 911** -911 is the telephone number that you can call for help. Fire fighters, police officers, and ambulance drivers can come and help if you call them. **Only use this number if you need help.**

Rule 5. **DO NOT TALK TO OR GO ANYWHERE WITH STRANGERS** Strangers are people that you do not know. You should not talk to or go anywhere with someone that you do not know. If a stranger wants you to go with them or wants to talk to you, you should **run away and tell an adult.**

Rule 6. **TELL YOUR PARENTS WHERE YOU ARE GOING** - If you want to go outside to play, or if you want to go over to a friend's house, always remember to tell your parents where you are going. If you leave your home and do not tell your parents where you are going, they will not know where you are. Your parents will worry and you will probably be in trouble.

Rule 7. **DO NOT TASTE ANYTHING, UNLESS YOU KNOW WHAT IT IS** - You should not eat or drink anything unless you know what it is. There are many things that look and smell good, but can be very bad for you. Ask your parents before you taste anything.

Rule 8. **NO ONE SHOULD TOUCH YOUR PRIVATE PARTS** - When your parents take you to the doctor for a check-up, your trusted doctor may need to check your private parts. You will need to touch your private parts when you take a bath or you may want to check your private parts. Your body belongs to you! No one has the right to touch you if you do not want to be touched. Do you know what your private parts are? They are the parts of your body that are covered by underwear.

SAFETY RULES

Rule 9. **ALWAYS WEAR A SEATBELT** - Wearing your seatbelt in the car is a very important rule. It will keep you safe in the car. When you get in a car put your seatbelt on right away. If the adults in the car forget to put on their seatbelts, REMIND THEM!

Rule 10. **BEWARE OF ANIMALS THAT YOU DO NOT KNOW** - Animals are our friends. If you have a pet, you know how much fun an animal can be BUT ... you should not touch or walk up to an animal that you do not know. Even a nice animal when it is scared may bite. Also remember, that you should never poke, hit or tease an animal.

Rule 11. **WHO CAN HELP IF YOU ARE LOST** - You will probably never get lost because you have learned to stay by your parents, friends or teachers when you are out. But it is a good idea to know who can help if you do get lost. Most places that children go are stores, libraries, zoos, and buildings where people work. If you are lost, find someone who works there. These people usually wear badges, smocks, stand behind a counter or a cash register. Police officers can help you too.

Rule 12. **DO NOT TOUCH ELECTRICAL OUTLETS** - We use electrical outlets for plugging in lamps, small appliances and things that need electricity. Nothing else should ever be put into an electrical outlet because it could seriously hurt you. Adults should plug cords into outlets. CHILDREN SHOULD NOT.

Rule 13. **DO NOT EAT UNKNOWN PLANTS** - Many of the foods we eat grow in gardens or on farms. These are good plants: beans, carrots, cucumbers, celery, etc. Some plants that may look good to eat are poisonous! Don't eat any plants except the ones you *know* are are okay to eat.

Rule 14. **PRACTICE FIRE ESCAPES** - You will probably never be in a building that is on fire. Just in case, you should know how to get out of a building that is on fire. Practicing how to get out of a building is called a "fire drill." Schools have fire drills. You should practice and have fire drills at home too. Remember what your teachers tell you to do at school and make fire escape plans at home with your family.

SAFETY RULES

Rule 15. **NO KITE FLYING BY POWER LINES** - Kite flying is fun, but can be dangerous if there are power lines nearby. Power lines carry electricity. If a kite gets caught in a power line, it could be very serious and you could be badly hurt. DO NOT FLY KITES NEAR POWER LINES.

Rule 16. **DO NOT PLAY IN WATER ALONE** - Water is tons of fun to play in. Lakes, oceans, ponds, rivers, swimming pools and even bath tubs provide great fun if an adult is with you. Children should never get into water unless an adult is near. Listen to adults and stay away from water unless an adult is with you.

Rule 17. **DO NOT RUN INTO THE STREET** - When you are playing outside, there are many types of toys that can roll into the street (balls, wagons, bikes, frisbees, etc.) Older children may be able to go into the street and get their own toy if they look both ways before they cross the street. Younger children may need to have an adult go into the street to get their toy. Know what you should do. Whatever your rule is, YOU SHOULD NEVER RUN INTO THE STREET!

Rule 18. **PLASTIC BAGS ARE DANAGEROUS** - There are many different kinds of plastic bags: dry cleaning bags, shopping bags, garbage bags, etc. They look like a lot of fun, but they are very dangerous. Children can get stuck in plastic bags. There is not any air in a plastic bag. You cannot breath in a plastic bag. If there are any old plastic bags in your house, you should tie knots in them before you throw them away so children will not be able to get inside of them or put them over their heads.

Rule 19. **STAY BY YOUR PARENTS** - When you are out grocery shopping, at the park, at a shopping center, or anywhere from your home, you should stay by your parents or the adult who is in charge. If you stay by the adults you are with, you will not get lost.

Activity: You may reproduce each of the safety rules on individual pieces of paper. The children can create a drawing to illustrate each of the rules. When the children have completed an illustration for each safety rule, the pages can be bound together in book form for the children to take home and share with their parents.

I can tell you my ADDRESS

_____

_____

_____

_____

Ask Me! _____
Date

I can tell you my PHONE NUMBER

_____
Date

_____

SAFETY ACTIVITIES

STOP AND GO

The children race around the gym or playground until the "stop" sign is held up by the teacher. The children wait for the "go" sign before resuming running. It is also fun to give the children the opportunity of being the police officer who is responsible for manipulating the traffic signs.

CROSSING THE STREET

Make an intersection in your classroom. Using tape on the floor works well to identify the boundaries of the street. Let the children take turns using a small whistle and helping the other children to cross the street. Encourage some fun dramatic play. Tell the police officer to watch for the cars and signal the traffic by using arms and giving directions. Some of the children may wish to pretend they are driving cars on the street.

STOP/DROP/ROLL

When the children are learning about fire fighters is a good time to introduce the safety rule, STOP/DROP/ROLL. Explain to the children that they will probably never be in a building that catches on fire, but it is a good idea to know what to do just in case.

Explain to the children that if their clothes caught on fire they should stop *(do not run, it will make the fire grow)*, drop on the ground and roll. Dropping on the ground and rolling will put the fire out. Children also think it is great fun to practice this safety rule.

SAFETY ACTIVITIES

STRANGERS

The topic of strangers can be handled well when you are discussing police officers with your class. For a young child, the concept of "what is a stranger?" is very difficult. Some children think that strangers are monsters, animals, or something that big people like to talk about. I think that teachers and parents can effectively talk about safety and strangers with their children in a simple manner. There are very few rules to remember:

1) Never go anywhere with someone that you do not know. Even if someone says that coming with them would be a lot of fun, or that your parents would want you to go, YOU SHOULD NEVER GO.

2) If a stranger approaches you, walk or run away. Do not stay and listen to what the stranger has to say. Go to the nearest house or building and tell an adult.

3) Teach children the difference between surprises and secrets. A surprise is something that will make someone happy; like a birthday present or a painting that you made at school. Secrets often do not make people happy. Children should never keep secrets. If someone asks you to keep a secret, you should always tell your parents or another adult that you trust.

Activity: Have the children role play various situations.
How do they handle being approached by a stranger?
Do the children know what to do?
Who are some of the trusted adults in a child's life?
Do the children know who they can go to for help?
Do the children understand the difference between a secret and a surprise?

DO NOT Talk to or Go Anywhere With Strangers

Strangers are people that you do not know. You should not talk to or go anywhere with someone you do not know. If a stranger (someone you do not know) wants you to go with them or wants to talk to you, you should walk or run away.

This child is walking away from a stranger. Good for this child. Color the child and give the child a happy face on this paper.

WHOOTIE GIVES A WHOOT!
(Medicines as Poisons)

Five year old Jenny Blake lived on a small farm in the country with her mother, father, and Pepper the puppy, Bucky the baby goat, Snowball the kitten, Patches the pony and Candy the calf.

The little girl and her animal friends had wonderful times together. They played hide-and-seek among the tall trees in the forest near the farm; rolled down the green velvety hills; and chased each other around the barn. And sometimes they were so noisy they woke up their friend, Whootie, the very wise Owl who lived in a huge tree near the barn. If he wasn't too sleepy, he would swoop down and join in the fun.

Very early one morning, just when the sun began to peek out from behind a fluffy white cloud, Pepper the puppy ran to the red barn. "Come on Bucky, hurry up!" he shouted as he passed by. Bucky the goat yawned and stretched. Then he hurried to catch up with Pepper. "Where are we going so early?" he asked. "I'm sleepy." Before he could answer, Snowball the kitten jumped out of a tree and landed on the ground in front of them. "What's the big hurry?" she asked. Again, before Pepper could explain, Patches the pony and Candy the calf came galloping up from the pasture and skided to a stop. "What's going on?"

"Jenny's in the hospital!" Pepper explained as fast as he could. "I heard her mother tell someone on the phone. She ate something she shouldn't have and it made her very sick! Wheww!"

With Pepper leading, they hurried toward the road to town. As they passed Whootie's tree, he woke up. "Whooo - what's all the commotion? I just went to sleep!"

"Jenny's in the hospital and we're all going to see her." Pepper, Snowball, Patches, Candy and Bucky said.

Whootie flew out of his tree and circled above them. "I'll go with you." And they all went as fast as they could. As soon as they reached the hospital, they each hurried to a different window looking for their playmate. "Here she is!" Patches finally called. There in the room they saw Jenny's mother and father standing beside the hospital bed, waiting anxiously as the doctor examined their little girl. He placed a stethoscope on her chest and listened to her heartbeat. Then he held her wrist and took her pulse. Finally the doctor nodded, pleased, "Your little girl will be alright now," he said to Jenny's parents. "You can take her home tomorrow."

"Yippee," Pepper yipped. "Hooray," Whootie hooted and he flapped his wings. Then they all hugged each other and jumped up and down. They were so happy.

But on the way home, Whootie became very quiet and serious. "What's wrong,

Whootie?" You should be happy Jenny's coming home tomorrow," Candy said. "That's right," the others agreed.

"I am," Whootie answered. "But I've been thinking. I really care about all of my friends - you and Jenny - and I'm worried that if you don't know what is safe to eat, you could get sick too, just like Jenny - or even worse!" "How are we going to know?" they wondered. Whootie began to speak.

"Well, I'll just have to teach you. And since I really do give a hoot, I'll give up an hour or two of my daytime sleep to hold a class, as soon as Jenny gets home."

The very first day that Jenny could go on and play, Patches gave her a ride to Whootie's tree where Snowball, Candy, and Bucky were waiting. "Where's Pepper?" Whootie asked. "Don't know," they answered.

Suddenly, Pepper came running out from behind the barn. "Sorry, I'm late," he panted. Then he quickly tried to hide something he was carrying in his mouth. Whootie perched on the lowest limb of his tree and peered over the easel standing in front of him. "What do you have there?" he asked Pepper. "Oh --- nothing," said Pepper.

"Pepper!" Whootie said firmly. Pepper sighed, "Well, okay." He gave it to Whootie.

"Why, this is a medicine bottle with some pills!" Whootie exclaimed. "Where did you get this Pepper?" asked Whootie. "Found it in the trash," Pepper mumbled. "Looked good enough to eat." Whootie frowned. Then he turned to the sheet of paper on the easel, and wrote in great big letters with a big black pen: MEDICINE IS NOT CANDY! Then he peered at his little friends, very solem. "Now, repeat after me - MEDICINE IS NOT CANDY! Even if it looks and tastes good. The right amount when you're sick and need it can make you better. But it also can make you very sick when you don't need it or if you take too much."

He turned the page on his easel and drew a picture of a bottle and wrote the word VITAMINS on the bottle. "Even vitamins," he said. "I know they look good and taste good and they are good for you, BUT only the amount your parents gives you. If you take too many, they can be very bad too, like medicine."

"Now," said Whootie, "What have you learned today?"

"Don't take more vitamins than your parents give you," Jenny said. "Medicine is not candy - even if it looks good and tastes good," Pepper and Snowball said. "Don't take medicine at all unless the doctor or your parents give it to you," they all answered together. "GOOD!" said Whootie, very pleased.

"Jenny, Jenny! Time for supper!" mother called from the back door of the farmhouse. "Pepper, Snowball, Everyone - your food is waiting!"

"Bye Whootie. We learned a lot."

"See you all tomorrow," Whootie called as they ran off.

From, Whootie, Gives A Hoot (Medicines as Poisons)
By Jacquie Milligan and Debra R. Scovel
Copyright © T.S. Denison & Co., Inc.

Name _____

Only Take Medicine/Vitamins From a Trusted Adult

The correct amount of medicine when you are sick can help you to feel better. Your parents or a trusted doctor will give the medicine to you. Too much medicine can make you very sick. CHILDREN SHOULD NEVER HELP THEMSELVES TO MEDICINE OR VITAMINS! Even if the medicine looks good and smells good you should not take it unless your parents have given it to you. If you find something that looks like a pill or medicine, give it to an adult right away. They will be proud of you.

MEDICINE CABINET

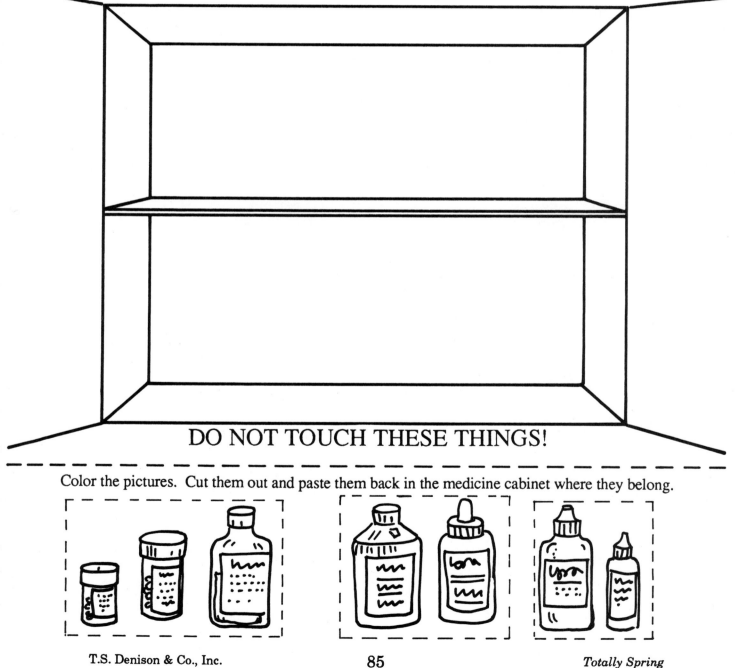

DO NOT TOUCH THESE THINGS!

Color the pictures. Cut them out and paste them back in the medicine cabinet where they belong.

T.S. Denison & Co., Inc.   85   *Totally Spring*

Is Your Home Poison-Proof?
A Checklist of Poisonous Products Found in the Home

Kitchen
- ☐ ammonia
- ☐ carpet & upholstery cleaners
- ☐ cleaning fluid
- ☐ cleansers & scouring powders
- ☐ drain cleaner
- ☐ furniture polish
- ☐ metal cleaners
- ☐ oven cleaner
- ☐ powder & liquid detergents
- ☐ prescription & non-prescription medicines
- ☐ rust remover

Bedroom
- ☐ cologne/perfume
- ☐ cosmetics
- ☐ jewelry cleaner
- ☐ sleeping medications

Garage, Basement, Workshop
- ☐ antifreeze
- ☐ epoxy glue
- ☐ fertilizer
- ☐ gasoline
- ☐ insecticides
- ☐ kerosene
- ☐ lighter fluid
- ☐ lime
- ☐ lye
- ☐ paint
- ☐ paint remover & thinner
- ☐ pesticides/garden sprays
- ☐ turpentine

Bathroom
- ☐ drain cleaner
- ☐ hair dyes
- ☐ hair remover
- ☐ nail polish & remover
- ☐ permanent wave solution
- ☐ pine oil & bath oil
- ☐ prescription & non-prescription medicines
- ☐ room deodorizer
- ☐ rubbing alcohol
- ☐ shampoo, wave lotion, sprays
- ☐ shaving lotion
- ☐ toilet bowl cleaner

General
- ☐ alcoholic beverages
- ☐ cigarettes
- ☐ flaking paint
- ☐ plants

Closets, Attic, Storage Places
- ☐ moth balls & sprays
- ☐ rat poison & ant poison

Purse
- ☐ cigarettes
- ☐ prescription & non-prescription medicines

Laundry
- ☐ bleach
- ☐ bluing, dyes
- ☐ disinfectants
- ☐ powder & liquid detergents

SMOKEY THE BEAR AND THE FOREST FIRE

This story happened not too long ago in a big forest. It was a very hot day and all of the forest animals were resting in the shade of the trees. One little bear cub which had left its mother to play in the meadow was the only forest creature stirring.

Then it happened! Some careless person flipped a lighted match, or left his campfire burning. A little flame started in the grass and began to burn. Quickly, it spread until the flame became a roaring forest fire.

The birds and other animals began to try to get away from the flames. They ran as fast as they could from the fire.

The fire jumped to the trees and began to spread even faster. Smoke from the fire filled the air. The men in the lookout tower spotted the forest fire and fire fighters rushed to the scene. But the flames were already so hot that the fire fighters could do nothing but lie down on the ground and cover their faces to keep from smothering.

When the fire was all over and the smoke had cleared, the forest did not look much like it had before. All of the trees and animals were gone — there were only burned stumps left.

The fire fighters got up and looked around, but they only saw one living thing — a badly burned little bear cub clinging to a burned tree limb. As the fire fighters carried the little cub through the forest that had been his home, what do suppose he saw? He saw the burned trees that would never again offer cool shade to the animals. How were the trees useful to people before they were burned? They had provided materials for homes, furniture, paper, and many other useful things.

The little cub saw that there was no grass. In what ways would this harm the life of the forest? There would be no grass to feed the animals or protect the soil from heavy rains. Could a lack of grass in the forest affect *us* in any way?

A very sad thing for the burned cub to see was the stream filled with ashes. What life in the forest depends on the streams? If the streams were no longer a good home for fish or a good drinking place for other animals, how would it affect us?

The fire fighters took the little cub home with them. They bandaged his burned feet and fed him baby food. And they gave the little cub a name — Smokey. Someone put a forest ranger's hat on his head and Smokey posed for many pictures. He also made personal appearances and appeared on television programs.

Smokey the Bear became a symbol for the prevention of forest fires. He is very famous. Smokey has a very important message for all of us. **Prevent Forest Fires!** What do you think he wants us to remember when we are in the forest? He wants us to be careful to put out campfires before we leave them — all the way out. How can we make sure a campfire is completely out? He also knows that children should never play with matches because they could very easily cause a destructive forest fire. Smokey wants to be sure that boys and girls will report a fire to someone if they see one. Children can even remind adults that are careless, if they do it in a nice way.

Above all, Smokey wants all of us to make certain that we are never the careless person who starts a forest fire that can destroy the animals, grass, trees, water and soil of the forest.

Use as a flannel board story. Patterns found on pages 88 & 89.
From Science Flannel Board Stories. By Vicki Hartwig. Copyright © T.S. Denison & Co., Inc.

STORY PATTERNS

Patterns for the story, "Smokey the Bear and The Forest Fire," found on page 87.

Squirrel

Fire Fighter

Ranger Hat

Grass (before the fire)

Small flame

Large flame

Bear Cub

STORY PATTERNS

Patterns for the story, "Smokey the Bear and The Forest Fire," found on page 87.

Forest trees (before fire)

Tree stump

Grass (after fire)

Smoke

Forest trees (after fire)

SAFETY BULLETIN BOARD

SAFETY AT SCHOOL

The teacher should cover the bulletin board with white paper. Divide the bulletin board into two sections. Write the caption "SAFETY IN THE CLASSROOM" in one section, and the caption 'SAFETY ON THE PLAYGROUND" in the other section. Discuss various safety rules with the children. As the children think of various rules, have the children illustrate the rule on the bulletin board. The teacher can print the rule under the child's drawing.

SAFETY MUSIC/RHYMES

SAFETY FIRST

We work. We shop. We play. We coast. We drive wagons. We ride bicycles. We walk. We swim. We run. Whatever we do, we must take care of ourselves and remember always: *safety first.*

In all my____ play At home or a-way, No mat-ter where I go, To cross the street, In crowds I meet, It is Safe-ty First I ____ have to know.

I look to the left, I look to the right, Be-fore I cross the street. And list-en when the traf-fic man Blows a whis-tle loud with a "Tweet, tweet, tweet."

Suggestion: Someone who has a whistle may blow it on the "Tweet, tweet, tweet" as we sing. March around the room, singing this marching song. One child may be the traffic officer and blow the whistle for the marchers to mark time and to start the marching again.

TRAFFIC ACTION PLAY

Standing on the corner in his blue uniform	*(standing tall)*
Watch the police officer tell the traffic what to do.	
This is stop.	*(one hand held up, palm out)*
This is go.	*(hand beckons)*
All the cars move to and fro.	*(move hands left and right)*
When he blows the whistle "To-weet! To-weet! To-weet!"	*(pretend to blow)*
The cars will stop.	*(hand held up for stop)*
Now - you can cross the street!	*(walk in place)*

CAUTION

Red says stop.	*(palm of hand up)*
Green says go.	*(hand beckons)*
You wait for yellow.	*(palm of hand up)*
It says go slow.	*(wave hand in slow motion)*
I always wait for mommy.	
When I cross the street.	
I take her hand and look both ways	*(look right and left)*
And my head tells my feet.	*(point to head and feet)*

SUGGESTED READING LIST

Chlad, Dorothy. ***Animals Can Be Special Friends.*** Children's Press. Copyright © 1985. *Summary:* Brief text and illustrations describe some of the rules for taking care of pets and treating animals at the zoo and in the wild.

Chlad, Dorothy. ***Bicycles Are Fun To Ride.*** Children's Press. Copyright © 1984. *Summary:* A young boy tells how he enjoys riding his bicycle while remembering important safety rules.

Chlad, Dorothy. ***Matches, Lighters, and Firecrackers.*** Children's Press. Copyright © 1982. *Summary:* Presents safety rules.

Chlad, Dorothy. ***Poisons Make You Sick.*** Children's Press. Copyright © 1984. *Summary:* A small girl named Tammy explains why one should never put strange things in one's mouth.

Chlad, Dorothy. ***Strangers.*** Children's Press. Copyright © 1982. *Summary:* Presents some rules for safe behavior around people you don't know.

Chlad, Dorothy. ***When I Cross The Street.*** Children's Press. Copyright © 1982. *Summary:* Presents safety rules when crossing the street.

Milligan, Jacquie. ***Child Safety Series.*** T.S. Denison & Co., Inc. Copyright © 1986. Titles in the series:
Whootie Gives a Hoot - Medicines as Poisons.
Spring Cleaning - Household Poisons
Marshmallow Autumn - Fire Safety
Potluck Picnic - Poisonous Plants
Lazy Day Adventure - Water Safety

MOTHER'S DAY AND FATHER'S DAY

CONTENTS

MOTHER'S DAY & FATHER'S DAY
GIFT IDEAS

SILHOUETTE CARD

Make a silhouette of child's head. Decrease to minature with pantograph. With rubber cement, paste it on to background of white construction paper, 3.5" x 4.5". Mount on inside of Mother's Day or Father's Day card with photo corners.

HAPPY MOTHER'S DAY

Here is a fun Mother's Day project that is not only attractive, but is also very useful. *You will need:* plastic "dixie" type cups or small flower pots for each child; plastic picnic forks; plaster of paris and plastic flowers.

Give each child a cup, flower and fork. Mix the plaster. Pour the plaster in each cup. Center the fork with the handle down in the plaster. Stick the stems of the flowers into the plaster. Let dry.

If you haven't already guessed you have created a ***recipe card holder.*** A recipe card will fit on the tines of the fork.

SACHET

The children cut a folded piece of pink construction paper into a rock shape, leaving the top fold uncut. With a paper punch, punch holes around the edges. Sew through the holes with yarn. A cotton ball sprinkled with talcum or perfume is taped inside. Tie yarn into bow when finished. This is a nice small gift that can be encloed in a card.

FATHER'S DAY PROJECT

To complete this Father's Day project you will need some help from the moms. Ask each of the moms to send to school with their child one of dad's white T-shirts. The children can personalize a T-shirt for their dad with this fabric paint recipe:

What you need: 1 cup of powdered albumen (or egg white); 3 cups of liquid tempera paint; and a few drops of vinegar.

What you do: Add one cup of powdered albumen to the three cups of liquid tempera paint. Add a few drops of vinegar. Apply colors to the fabric freely with stiff paint brush. To set the colors, place the cloth face down between two pieces of paper and steam with an iron.

MOTHER'S DAY & FATHER'S DAY
GIFT IDEAS

NAPKIN HOLDER

You will need: 1 quart plastic bottle; felt-tip markers; glue; sequins or other scrap fabric to decorate the napkin holder.

What you do: Wash each plastic bottle carefully and thoroughly. Cut the plastic bottle in half as shown in the illustration. The top section of the bottle is to be disgarded or saved for future art projects. The lower half of the bottle will be the napkin holder. Cut a vertical strip down each side an inch and a half wide. Cut this to within an inch from the bottom of the bottle.

Round the corners of each side and decorate with the markers or any other materials that you have found.

DOOR STOP CAT

You will need: one soft-drink bottle; 3 inch styrofoam ball; black enamel; paintbrush; sand or gravel; glue; two white buttons or moveable eyes; felt; one small rhinestone button.

What you do: Fill the bottle with sand or gravel. With a knife, the teacher should cut a hole in the styrofoam ball about as large as the mouth of the bottle. Put some glue in the hole and insert the neck of the bottle, pressing down on the styrofoam until it is glued in place. Paint the bottle and the attached ball with black enamel. When the paint is dry, glue on the eyes and the rhinestone button as a nose. The mouth and ears can be cut from felt and glued on. Adding a collar made from felt is a nice extra touch for the cat.

FABRIC FLOWER POT

Each child will need a small clay flower pot. Ask the children to bring to school a variety of print scrap fabric. Use pinking sheers and cut the fabric into small squares. Using white glue, have the children glue the fabric squares onto the outside of the flower pot.

When the squares have dried, have the children paint white glue all over the flower pot. When the glue is dry is will provide a shiny coating.

It makes an extra nice gift when the children plant a small flower in the pot to take home to their parents.

A SPECIAL COUPON BOOK FOR

_____

WITH LOVE, _____

Good for clearing the dinner table

Good for one back rub

Good for one giant hug

Good for emptying the wastepaper baskets

Good for 3 good-night kisses

Directions: Reproduce page 96 and 97 for each child in your class. Have the children cut out the coupons and staple all the coupons together in the upper left corner. The children can illustrate and decorate each of the coupons pages and the cover of the coupon book.

Good for making the beds

Good for picking up my room without being asked!

Good for not arguing with my brother/sister

Good for: *(your choice)*

_____

_____

_____

Good for an after dinner walk with you

Good for: *(your choice)*

_____

_____

_____

Directions: Reproduce page 96 and 97 for each child in your class. Have the children cut out the coupons and staple all the coupons together in the upper left corner. The children can illustrate and decorate each of the coupons pages and the cover of the coupon book.

MOTHER'S DAY STORY

TAMMIE'S GIFT OF LOVE

Tammie watched her older sister wrap a gift. Her sister, Ann, had painted a beautiful picture for a Mother's Day gift for their Mother.

"I wish I could paint a pretty picture for Mother," said Tammie.

"What are you going to give Mother?" asked Ann.

"I don't know," said Tammie.

The next two days Tammie thought and thought about what she could give her Mother for Mother's Day. She was too small to make something like Ann had made. But she wanted to show her Mother how much she loved her.

On Mother's Day, Tammie awakened early. She still hadn't decided what gift to give her Mother. She was very sad. She leaned on her window sill and looked outside.

"I want to show Mother that I love her," she thought.

As she was thinking, Tammie smelled a sweet fragrance. Near her window beautiful roses were blooming. Suddenly, Tammie smiled happily. She ran from her room and out the front door. She clipped a beautiful yellow rose bud from the bush and took it inside.

In the kitchen, she found a bud vase and placed the rose inside. Tammie ran excitedly to her Mother's room. Her Mother opened her eyes and smiled at her little daughter.

"Happy Mother's Day," said Tammie. "I love you."

"Oh, how beautiful," said her Mother. "I shall enjoy the sweet smell of this flower for days. What a lovely gift."

Tammie smiled. She was pleased that she had made her Mother so happy.

(Ask the children if they have something special planned for Mother's Day. Suggest some helpful tasks that the children could do for their mothers, or a type of gift that a young child could make or find.)

MOTHER'S DAY & FATHER'S DAY
RHYMES/POETRY

I'M JUST A LITTLE ONE
Have the children decorate a card to go with a gift that the children have made at school. Here is a nice verse that can be added to the inside of a card.
Though I'm just a little one,
I wanted you to know.
Today's your very special day,
And I love you so!

FATHER'S DAY (or Mother's Day)
On this very special day,
I wanted you to know,
You're the best dad (or mom) in all the world,
And I love you so!

MOTHERS
Mothers feed the baby	*(feed doll)*
Mothers cook and bake	*(open oven)*
Mothers put us in our beds	*(head on hand)*
And tell us when to wake	*(wake up)*

(Use this rhyme for fathers too!)

TAKING A WALK
When Dad and I go walking,	
His steps are long and so,	*(long exaggerated steps)*
I have to keep on running,	
As fast as I can go.	*(quick run)*
He steps across the puddles	
With one big step, while I	*(long steps)*
Jump straight across on both my feet	
Because he lifts me high	*(broad jump with both feet)*

Draw a picture of your Mom.

Draw a picture of your Dad

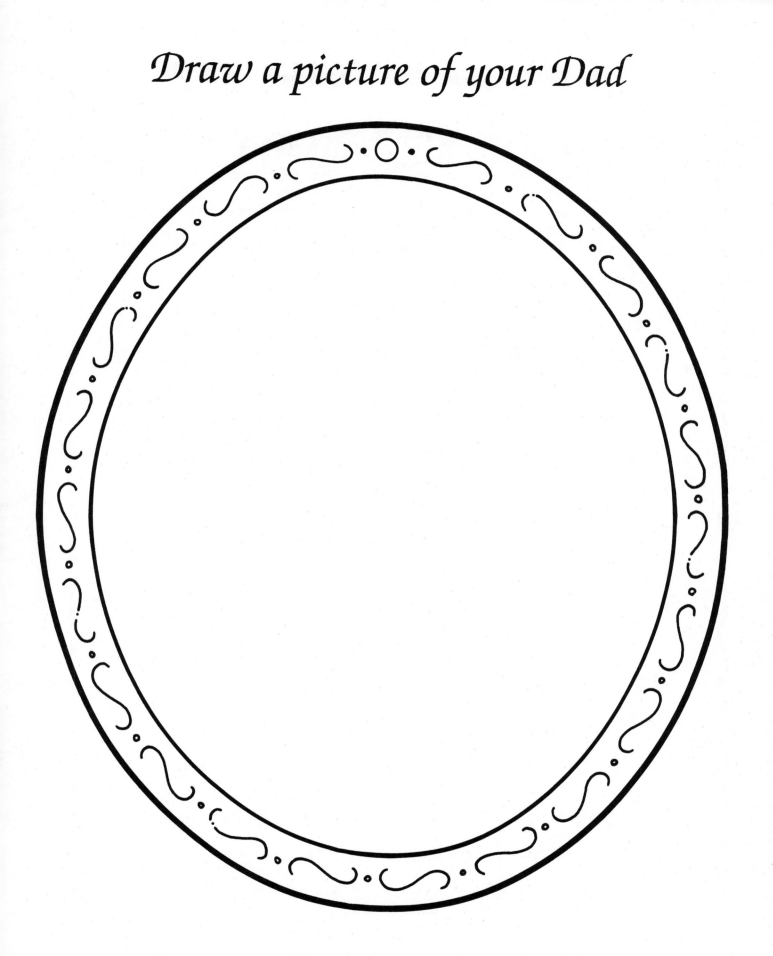

Written by:

This story is all about MY MOM

_____

_____

_____

_____

_____

_____

_____

_____

_____

_____

_____

Written by:

This story is all about MY DAD

_____

- -

_____

- -

_____

- -

_____

- -

_____

- -

_____

- -

_____

- -

_____

SUGGESTED READING LIST

Balian, Lorna. ***Mother's Mother's Day.*** Abingdon. Copyright © 1982.
Summary: Hazel the Mouse goes to visit her mother on Mother's Day, but finds she has gone to visit her mother.

Bunting, Eve. ***The Mother's Day Mice.*** Clarion Books. Copyright © 1986.
Summary: Three little mouse brothers go into the meadow to find a present for their mother but it is the littliest mouse that comes up with the most unusal gift of all.

Kroll, Steven. ***Happy Father's Day.*** Holiday House. Copyright © 1988.
Summary: Each of the children and mom have a special surprise for Dad on his special day.

Kroll, Steven. ***Happy Mother's Day.*** Holiday House. Copyright © 1985.
Summary: One day when mom returns home she is greeted by surprise after surprise from each of her six children and husband.

Sharmat, Marjorie Weinman. ***Hooray for Father's Day.*** Holiday House. Copyright © 1987. *Summary:* Father mule's two loving children spend Father's Day showering him with lovely presents that leave him exhausted, when the gift he really needs is a dose of peace and quiet.

Sharmat, Marjorie Weinman. ***Hooray for Mother's Day.*** Holiday House. Copyright © 1986. *Summary:* In searching for a Mother's Day present that will be just right, chicken demonstrates that he is just as cautious and particular as she is.

CELEBRATING GRANDPARENTS

CONTENTS

GRANDPARENT LEARNING ACTIVITIES

MY GRANDPARENTS

Ask the children to tell about their Grandparents. If there are children in the room who do not have any Grandparents, ask them if they have any older adults, such as a neighbor, aunt or uncle, who may be important to them. What makes their Grandparents so special? What types of activities do they enjoy doing with their Grandparents? What types of games, activities, and toys did the children's Grandparents play with when they were children.

WE BEGIN AS BABIES

It is often difficult for young children to believe that their Grandparents were ever babies. It can be helpful to discuss with the children how all living things begin life as babies. Here are some suggestions:

Every living thing begins life as a baby. Animal babies often have different names from the grown-up animals. For example, baby horses are called foals, baby cows are called calves, baby kangaroos are called joeys, and baby cats are called kittens.

Some animals look very different when they are babies from the way that they will look as they grow up. Caterpillars are baby butterflies, and you know how different a caterpillar looks from a butterfly. Most animals don't change this much as they grow up, though. Human babies really look pretty much like grown-ups. They are smaller, of course, and they aren't able to take care of themselves until they get bigger.

Note: End this activity by providing the children with the experience of matching pictures of baby animals to pictures of adult animals.

BABY PICTURES

Have each child bring a baby picture of themself. Tell them to bring the pictures in an envelope so no one else will see it. Put each child's name on the back of his/her picture. Place the pictures on a bulletin board. Allow the children several days to study the pictures. Then ask them who they think is in each picture. Record their votes on chart paper and compare the answers for a math activity. Reveal the identies of the children in the pictures and see who guessed correctly. Take pictures of the children and compare their recent pictures to their baby pictures.

GRANDPARENT GIFT IDEAS

A PICTURE OF GRANDMA AND GRANDPA

Have the children draw pictures of their grandparents. *(You may wish to use the reproducible activity provided on page 109.)* Put the picture in a picture frame that stands up. This is easily done by gluing the drawing on a piece of colored construction paper and attaching a tagboard brace to the back of the picture. *(See illustration.)* The Grandparents will be delighted with their grandchild's interpretation of what they look like. The picture will probably get a very prominent place in their home.

A BOOK ABOUT ME

This project will take the children a couple of weeks to complete for their Grandparents. It is more effective to have the children complete one page a day, rather than trying to do too many pages at once. Below are some suggestions for each page in the "A Book About Me." The children's Grandparents will be thrilled with this treasure. It will be cherished for years.

1. My name is ... and this is a picture of me.
2. This is my house.
3. This is a picture of my Mom and Dad.
4. This is a picture of my Grandparents. They are special to me because ...
5. This is a picture of my brother/sister.
6. These are my friends. We like to play ...
7. When I grow up, I want to be ...
8. If I could have one wish, I would wish for ...
9. Sometimes I am afraid of ...
10. This is a picture of some of my favorite things.
11. Put a photograph of the child on the last page and a cover on the front of the book.

Interview Your Grandparent(s)
(or a special older person in your life)

Person interviewed: _____ *Written by:* _____

1. When you were a child, what types of toys did you play with?

2. When you were a child what were some of your favorite school activities?

3. When you were a child, what types of clothes did you wear to school?

4. When you were a child, what type of music did you listen to?

5. What is one of your very favorite childhood memories?

My Grandparent/s

ILLUSTRATED BY _____

A GROWING-UP STORY

AS WE GROW

See the baby dressed in blue?
At nine months old, what can he
    do?
Can you find him among the
    others?
He's the smallest of all the
    brothers.

See the toddler all decked out.
He's a cowboy, without a doubt.
Can you find him among the
    others?
He's next in line of all the
    brothers.

See the girl with books in hand?
At five, she's bound for Kinder
    Land.
Can you see the sisters all?
Find this one, who is so small.

See the boy with the bat and ball?
He loves T-ball, but that's not all.
Can you find him among the
    others?
He's the middle of all the brothers.

See the girl with roller skates on?
Better look quick or she'll be gone.
Can you see the sisters all?
Find this one who is getting tall.

See the girl who leads the cheers?
When she yells, everyone hears!
Can you see the sisters all?
Find this one who is so tall.

See the boy who plays football?
He's the strongest of them all.
Can you find him among the
    others?
He's the oldest of the brothers.

See the girl who looks so glad?
She's about to become a grad.
As you grow up, and then look
    back,
You'll find yourself among this
    pack!

*(Use the patterns on pages 111 & 112
and make a family for the flannel board.
As you read the poem, put the characters
on the flannel board.)*

*From Beginning Science - The Essential Elements
By Kathy Morrison & Alice Reader
© T.S. Denison & Inc. Inc.*

STORY PATTERNS

Patterns for the story, "As We Grow," found on page 110.

Cheerleader

5 Year Old

Graduate

Toddler

STORY PATTERNS

Patterns for the story, "As We Grow," found on page 110.

Football Player

Girl on Skates

Baby in blue

T-Ball Player

OUR GRANDPARENTS ARE SPECIAL

Give each child a small paper plate (a cake-sized plate). Using yarn, markers, buttons, sequins, crayons, scrap fabric, or anything else that you may have on hand, let the children decorate the plates to look like their Grandparents. Display the paper plate Grandparents on the bulletin board, with the caption, "OUR GRANDPARENTS ARE SPECIAL." Have the bulletin board ready for that special day that the Grandparents are invited to school. Ask each of the Grandparents to find their face on the bulletin board.

GRANDPARENTS MUSIC/POETRY

IN GRANDMA'S DAY

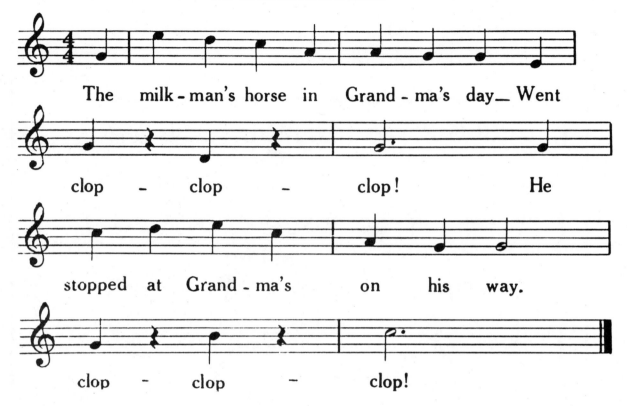

The milk-man's horse in Grand-ma's day— Went

clop - clop - clop! He

stopped at Grand-ma's on his way.

clop - clop - clop!

GRANDMOTHER'S SPECTACLES

Here are Grandmother's spectacles
      (make circles around eyes with thumb and forefinger)
Here is Grandfather's cap. *(make hands come together in peak on top of head)*
And this is the way they fold their hands
      (fold the hands)
And lay them in their lap
      (lay hands in lap)

A SPECIAL PLACE

I have a special place,
Where I get to go and play.
It is filled with laughter,
And I like to stay all day.

The people in this place,
Have the best surprises you ever saw.
And all I have to do is say,
Oh please, Grandma and Grandpa!

(Discuss playing at Grandma and Grandpa's house. What types of activities can you do at your Grandparent's house?)

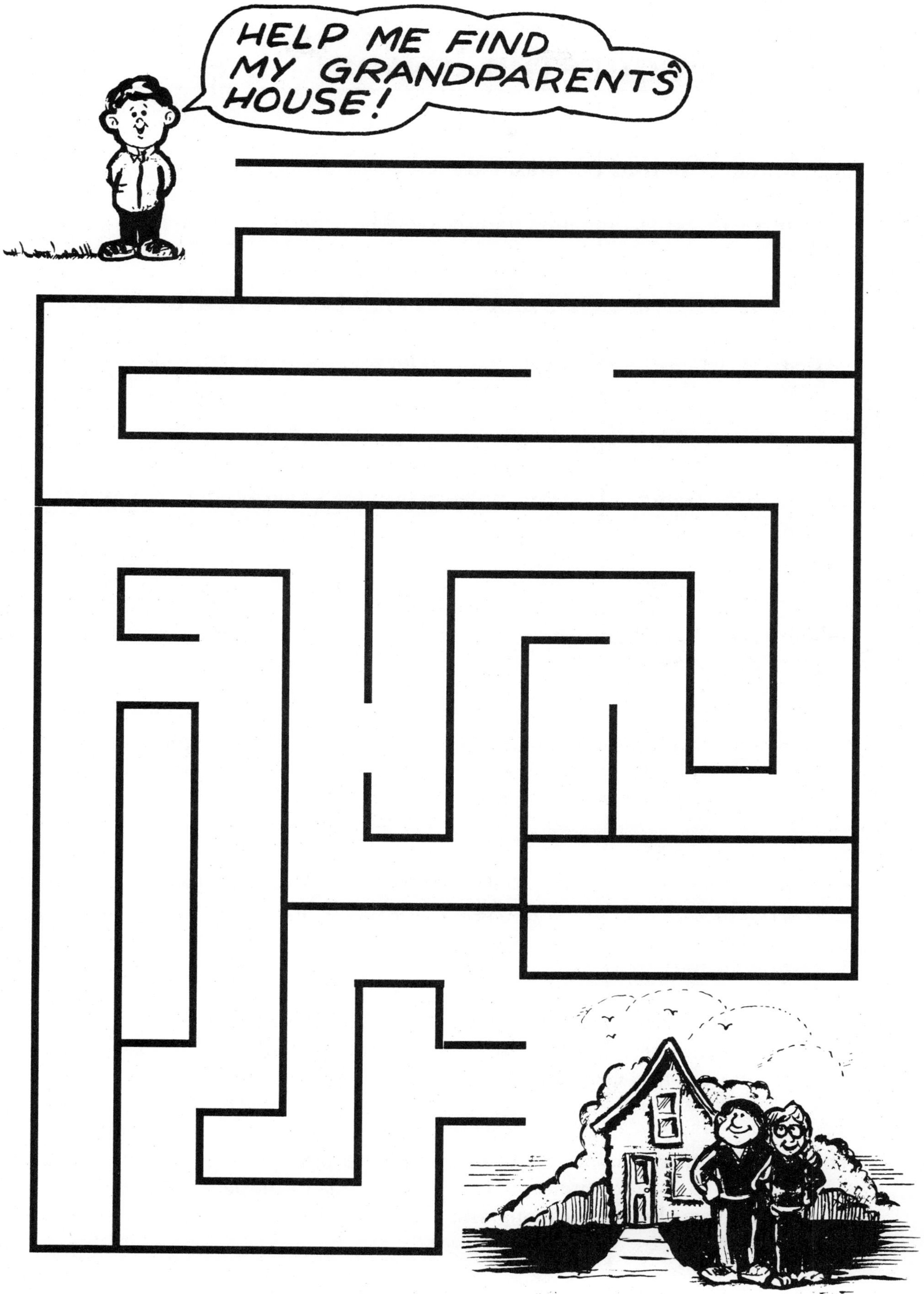
HELP ME FIND MY GRANDPARENTS' HOUSE!

SUGGESTED READING LIST

Asch, Frank. ***Milk and Cookies.*** Parent's Magazine Press. Copyright © 1982. *Summary:* While spending the night at Grandfather's house, baby bear dreams of feeding milk and cookies to a dragon.

Berenstain, Stan. ***The Berenstain Bears and the Week at Grandmas.*** Random House. Copyright © 1986. *Summary:* When Brother and Sister Bear get left with their Grandparents for a whole week, they have a better time than they expected.

Hooker, Ruth. ***At Grandma and Grandpa's House.*** A Whitman. Copyright © 1986. *Summary:* At Grandma and Grandpa's house there are always special things to see and do.

Hurd, Edith Thatcher. ***I Dance In My Red Pajamas.*** Harper and Row. Copyright © 1982. *Summary:* A young girl visits her Grandparents who feel the best day is a noisy day.

Kroll, Steven. ***Toot! Toot!*** Holiday House. Copyright © 1983. *Summary:* While playing with his toy train set, a young boy imagines he is going on a visit to his grandparent's farm.

Newman, Shirlee Petkin. ***Tell Me Grandma, Tell Me Grandpa.*** Houghton. Copyright © 1979. *Summary:* As a youngster hears about her parents when they were young, she turns her imagination loose.

Rockwell, Anne. ***When I Go Visiting.*** Macmillian Publishing. Copyright © 1984. *Summary:* A child describes a thoroughly enjoyable visit with her Grandmother and Grandfather in their city apartment.

Whitlock, Susan Love. ***Donovan Scares the Monsters.*** Greenwillow Books. Copyright © 1987. *Summary:* While visiting his grandparents, Donovan searches their house for monsters, which he scares away with their help.

BUGS, FROGS & TURTLES

CONTENTS

CREATING AN INSECT ZOO
FOR THE CLASSROOM AND OTHER FUN CREATURES!

Most young children enjoy looking for, catching, housing and feeding any type of small insect. So, muster up some courage and let your little ones create an exciting Insect Zoo. Here are some tips on how to find, feed and house all your bugs!

ANTS - Place in a minature vivarium, tight fitting top. Set in a saucer of water moat to prevent escape. Feed them sugar, honey. One drop of honey will feed 50 ants. Try bits of vegetable, fruit and bread crumbs. Use a piece of cardboard as a dish. Replace cardboard every other day. Try to keep balance between lack of water and too much water. Don't overfeed and avoid direct sunlight.

CATERPILLARS - Keep them in an insect glass jar with a screened top. Provide them with plenty of fresh leaves from the plant on which they were found. Sprinkle the leaves with moisture each day. Provide twigs for caterpillars to attach pupal stage to.

CRICKETS - Keep in a screened insect cage or jar with inch or two of damp sand in bottom. They will eat dead insects, bread, lettuce, apples, meat scraps, Moist piece of cotton for water supply. Provide some hiding places. Keep crickets separated. They are cannibalistic.

FROGS - Keep your frogs in a semi-aquatic aquarium with slopping mud banks, rocks that protrude above the water. Frogs will eat live mosquitoes, mealworms, flies, earthworms; may eat hamburger tied to a string and moved before eyes. Keep water at room temperature.

GARDEN SNAILS - Keep them in a fish bowl or glass jar; wire screen cover, seedlings planted in layer of damp soil. They will eat bits of lettuce, flower petals, celery leaves, dry bread. Keep in a cool, shady place. Keep jar moist but not soggy.

GRASSHOPPERS - Keep in a screened cage or terrarium. They will eat leaves, lettuce, dipped in water. They will die in the late fall after mating and laying eggs.

KATYDIDS - These should be cared for exactly like grasshoppers. They will also die in the late fall.

PRAYING MANTIS - Keep these in a screened cage or terrarium. They will eat a lot of insects; fruit flies, aphids. Spray with water each day. Separate adult mantis since they are cannibalistic.

SALAMANDERS - Keep in a shoreline aquarium or a clean jar with some pond water and pond plants. Cover tightly with screen. They will eat live insects, fruit flies, small earthworms, raw fish, raw liver, tiny pieces of egg white. They must have living moving food. Might remove salamander to dish filled with water to feed. You can condition a salamander to expect food when you tap on the side of the dish.

Classroom Animal Homes

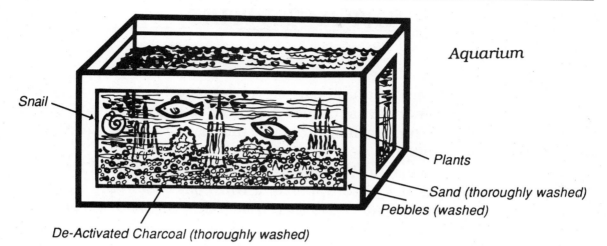

Aquarium

Snail

Plants

Sand (thoroughly washed)

Pebbles (washed)

De-Activated Charcoal (thoroughly washed)

Woodland Terrarium

Jar Lid

Low Woodland Plants

2-3 Inches Potting Soil

Pebbles, Gravel
De-Activated Charcoal

Gauze or screen

Water Insect Home

Pond water

Water plants

Pebbles,
washed sand

Temporary Insect Home

Container lid with
holes punched in it

Plastic sandwich
bag liner

Masking tape to
secure liner
to carton

Two or three "windows" cut from
container for viewing
animals

From The Curiosity Shop (A Sciencing Sampler for the Primary Years)
By Jane Goldman. © T.S. Denison & Co., Inc.

Totally Spring

BUGS, FROGS AND TURTLE
ART ACTIVITIES

ANTS

Ants are a natural part of warmer weather, and are common uninvited visitors at picnics. Many children are intrigued by ants - they are fun to watch, they build interesting houses, and they are easy to catch.

Using the illustration next to this activity, teach the children how to draw a picture of an ant. Draw one oval in the center of a piece of paper. Add three legs on each side. Draw an oval above the first circle, touching, and an oval below the first circle, also touching. Add antennae on top and two eyes.

CATERPILLAR

Young children love to use glue. This is an easy project that will provide your children with immediate success. Provide each of the children with 8 circles, each a different color. *(Older children may wish to cut out their own circles.)* Have the children glue the circles together in a long line to form the caterpillar. Pipe cleaners make nice antennae. When the caterpillar is complete the children can use him to name all the colors or to learn how to read the color words.

BUTTERFLY

After you have made the caterpillar, it is nice to discuss that caterpillars turn into butterflies. Provide the children with some templates of butterflies. Slip these under a piece of newsprint and color over them with a crayon used edgewise.

BUGS, FROGS AND TURTLE
ART ACTIVITIES

JUMPING FROG

In the spring, frog eggs are hatching and tadpoles are developing into frogs. Children really enjoy watching the development of frogs. If possible, bring some frog eggs into your classroom, so the children can have this experience.

Enlarge the frog patterns found next to this activity. Have the children either color or paint the frog and cut it out. Fold the frog in half and attach a string in the center of the frog's back. The children can use the frog as a puppet and make him (or her) hop.

TURTLE HAND PUPPET

Each child in the class will need two paper plates. Cut one of the paper plates in half. The half plate will be stapled on the back of the whole plate. *(Follow the illustration.)* This provides the space for the child to put his/her hand. Paint the whole paper plate green, and add legs and a turtle's head made from construction paper.

PAINTED BUTTERFLY

You will need: 12" x 18" white construction paper; black paper; tempera paint, blue, orange, yellow, and red; Q-tips; small pie tins.

What you do: The teacher will need to pre-cut a white butterfly shape and black body for younger children. Older will be able to cut out their own butterfly shape and black body. Pour different paint into each pie tin. Give each child a white butterfly and a Q-tip. Demonstrate how to 'dot' paint onto the butterfly. Trade Q-tips and pie tins until each child has used all the spring colors. When the butterfly has dried, glue on the body.

A FROG STORY

TEETO, THE TADPOLE

Teeto, the tadpole, was born in a large pond with many other little tadpoles. One day his mother went to the edge of the pond and laid her eggs in the cool water. The eggs floated in great green masses near the top of the water.

Each egg was small, round and light-colored. A black speck showed on each one. The eggs had grown and now polliwogs were hatching out of them. Teeto was a fat little polliwog. He wiggled and twisted to get out of his egg. He wanted to free himself.

The little fat polliwog got himself free at last and swam around. To his surprise, things began to grow upon him, making him look different. In a few days he had some gills on each side of his head. He could breathe through these. He had a fine tail for swimming, too, and could speed through the water much faster each day. Teeto was very proud of himself and was having such fun with his pals.

Best of all, though, were two little horns or beaks around his mouth. "Ah," he said to himself, "Just watch me eat and grow now." Sure enough, the two little beaks were very good for nipping off the green things floating in the pool, and for gobbling up mouthfuls of the mud that had tiny bits of good food in it. "I have to eat and grow," said little Teeto. "I can't be a polliwog all my life. I'm going to be something much grander."

He grew and grew. After a few weeks he became a full-grown tadpole. He was still very small, but fat and strong. Then it was time for him to change. His gills and tail began to disappear and little legs began to grow. "Good-bye gills and tail," said the little tadpole, "I like my strong legs much better."

Soon he became a small, green frog, with lovely big, wide open eyes and a very large mouth for such a little fellow. He had smooth, moist skin with lovely spotted colors. Behind his eyes were smooth drumheads that were his ears. He could hear and see very well, indeed. But he could eat best of all. He ate and ate. He liked worms, flies, mosquitos and other little insects that came his way.

And now he could jump and swim and dive! He certainly was glad that he no longer was an egg, or a polliwog, or a mere tadpole. He loved being a grown-up frog and even changed his name from TEETO, THE TADPOLE to FREDDY THE FROG.

(Patterns for the flannel board are provided on page 123. Older children may enjoy designing their own patterns to illustrate the story.)

From Story Telling with the Flannel Board, Book One.
By Paul Anderson.
Copyright by the T.S. Denison & Co., Inc.

STORY PATTERNS

Patterns for the story, "Teeto, the Tadpole," found on page 122.

BUGS, FROGS AND TURTLE RHYMES/POETRY

TURTLE RACE

I have two little turtles.   *(hands fisted, held frontwards for turtles)*
I keep them in a pan. *(left hand turtle pokes middle finger knuckle out for head)*
One turtle's name is Dick.
The other's name is Dan.   *(right hand turtle does the same)*

I built a diving platform
Over their swimming place.
My turtles, Dick and Dan,   *(hold out turtles one by one, left and then right turtle)*
Are going to have a race!

On your mark, turtles!   *(hold up turtles close to body infront of chest)*
Ready, set, go!   *(on "go," start them moving forward, slowly)*
Oh, my, Dan,
You really are slow!   *(left hand turtle move ahead a little)*

Look out, Dick!   *(right hand turtle catches up - moves ahead)*
Dan is going to win!
No - I think that Dick   *(left hand turtle - middle finger snaps out)*
Will be the first one to dive in!

Oh, Dick has stopped!   *(right hand turtle catches up)*
He's snapping at a fly!
Funny little turtles   *(both turtles dive downwards at same time)*
It's a tie!

THE FROG

A funny little frog   *(stooping)*
Hopped up on a log   *(hop up and forward)*
Then like a flash   *(jump back down)*
Jumped down, kersplash!

THE LITTLE FROGGIES

One little, two little,
Three little froggies,
Four little, five little,
Six little froggies.
Seven little, eight little,
Nine little Froggies.
Ten little froggies,
Jumping in the pond.
(Sing and as you say this
rhyme children jump in
the pond.)

THE TURTLE

This is my turtle
     (make fist, extend thumb)
He lives in a shell.
     (hide thumb)
He likes his home very well.
He pokes his head out.
     (extend thumb)
When he wants to eat,
And then he pulls it back,
     (hide thumb)
When he wants to sleep.

INSECT BULLETIN BOARD

INSECTS

This is a fun bulletin board for the children to make, but it is also a good table display. Have the children make insects by pasting and bending pipecleaners to make six legs. Construction paper bodies and heads can be added to the legs. Provide the children with a multitude of materials so they create their own insects with some imagination.

If you display the insects on a table top, add real stones, rocks, and grass for an added special effect. If you pin the insects to a bulletin board you can also add construction paper grass, rocks, etc to your "insect scene."

SUGGESTED READING LIST

Freeman, Don. ***The Chalk Box Story.*** Lippincott. Copyright © 1976.
Summary: Pieces of colored chalk draw a story about a boy stranded on
an island and is resued by a turtle.

Galdone, Paul. ***The Frog Prince.*** McGraw. Copyright © 1975. *Summary:*
Adapted from the retelling of The Brothers Grimm.

Hoff, Syd. ***Palace Bug***. Putnam. Copyright © 1970. *Summary:* No one
recognizes the little bug's devotion to the king until he appears on top of
the king's dinner plate.

Kalan, Robert. ***Jump Frog Jump.*** Greenwillow Books. Copyright © 1981.
Summary: A cummulative tale in which a frog tries to catch a fly without
being caught itself.

Lobel, Arnold. ***Frog and Toad are Friends.*** Harper. Copyright © 1970.
Summary: Five tales recounting the adventures of two best friends - Frog
and Toad.

Lobel, Arnold. ***Grasshopper on the Road.*** Harper. Copyright © 1978.
Summary: As grasshopper sets out to follow a road he meets some unusal
characters.

McKissack, Pat. ***Bugs!*** Children's Press. Copyright © 1988. *Summary:*
Simple text and illustrations of a variety of insects introduce the numbers
one through five.

Murdocca, Sal. ***Turtle's Shell.*** Lothrop. Copyright © 1976. *Summary:* When
Tuttle, the turtle loses his shell, his animal friends help him trick Louis
the rat into giving it back.

Soya, Kiyoshi. ***The House of Leaves.*** Philomel Books. Copyright © 1987.
Summary: Sheltering from the rain, Sarah shares a house of leaves with
praying mantis, ladybug and other small creatures of the wild.

UNDERWATER ANIMALS

CONTENTS

Underwater Animal Art Activities

AQUARIUM

You will need: Large family-sized cereal box; scissors; tape; string; piece of plastic; drawing paper or material scraps.

What you do: Tape top flaps down. Cut a window in the front leaving a half-inch frame around the front. Draw different kinds of fish, eel, seahorse, etc. Punch a hole in each. Tie different lengths of string to them and tape the other end of the string to the underside of the top. Tape or paste a piece of plastic over the front opening behind the frame. It gives the illusion of water in a glass aquarium. For added realism, make sea creatures from pieces of material and stuff them with other scraps. Paint pebbles and scatter them on the floor of the aquarium. Cut seaweed from green construction paper and add between the pebbles at the bottom.

MOSAIC FISH

Give each of the children a light blue piece of construction paper, with the shape of a fish drawn on it. *(Older children will be able to draw their own fish.)* The children should tear small pieces of colored construction paper, and paste on the fish to represent scales.

FISH CRACKER FUN

Give each of the children a cut-out of a fish bowl or have the children draw and cut out their own fish bowl shape. *(See illustration for an example of the shape of a fish bowl.)* Have the children draw seaweed, a fish house, gravel for the bottom of the bowl; anything which they think will "dress-up" the fish bowl. When the bowl is finished let the children glue "fish-shaped" crackers onto their bowls. *(These crackers are available at most grocery stores. One box should be enough for your entire class.)*

Underwater Animal World

Draw as many different kinds
of fish as you can.
Use many different colors.

Name _____

UNDERWATER ANIMAL
LANGUAGE ACTIVITIES

FACTS ABOUT FISH

Fish are animals that live in water. There are many different kinds of fish, and they live in all parts of the world. Some fish live in lakes, some live in rivers, and others live in the oceans. How do fish breath if they are always in water?

a) People breathe through their noses.

b) Fish have gills. Gills cannot use the oxygen in the air that we breathe. Fish breathe the water by taking it in at the mouth, letting it flow over the gills and out the opening behind the gill covers.

c) In people the air goes in the nose and through the lungs. Then it goes out the nose.

UNDERWATER ANIMAL PROJECT

On a large table, have the children make the ocean bottom. Sand and plants should be available for them to use. Make clay models of animals that live in the water *(fish, lobsters, crabs, snails, etc.)* or animals that may live near the water *(seals, turtles, frogs, etc.)* Give each child a ball of clay and toothpicks. The toothpicks may be used to make legs or to hold on the head of an animal. Crinkle several sheets of blue paper. Place these on the table to create the ocean water. Sprinkle sand around the water. As each child finishes his animal, he may place it in the water or near it. Leave this display up for at least a few days. Whenever a child has some free time, he may make more animals for the display.

MAGNIFYING GLASS

Ask the children to bring things from home that have come from under the water: shells, coral, seahorse, etc. Allow the children to take part in the discussion of these treasures. Talk about plant life at the bottom of the oceans, lakes, rivers.

Leave all the treasures that the children have brought to school on a table. *(They would add nicely to the UNDERWATER ANIMAL PROJECT listed above.)* Let the children examine all the objects with a magnifying glass. Each child is instructed to notice something about a specimen and not tell anyone. The children can then tell their observations and see how many noticed the same things.

UNDERWATER ANIMAL GAMES

THE FISHING GAME

Make a fishing game for a corner of your classroom while you are studying life underwater. Make the fish from construction paper. Attach paper clips to each fish. Make fishing poles with sticks (or rulers) and string, and tie magnets to the end of the string. You can use this game to teach almost anything.

1. Spelling words
2. Sight word vocabulary
3. Colors and shapes
4. Alphabet letters and numbers
5. Animals and objects
6. Addition and subtraction facts
7. Creative writing assignments (each fish would have a task written on it)
8. Independent activities

THROW BACK THE FISH

Cut one large hole in a big box. Draw or paint waves on the box to represent the water. Give the children bean bags and tell the children to pretend that the bean bags are fish. All these fish are too small to keep, so they must be thrown back into the water. Have the children toss the bean bags into the hole in the box. As the children gain more confidence, move the box back farther.

FISH RACES

Talk about how fish move in the water; they swim, move smoothly, etc. Talk about how fish move when they are out of water; they wiggle, jump, flop around. Have the children run races moving the way fish do. Pretend that some are in water, and during some of the races the fish are out of the water.

The Goldfish Bowl

Directions: Cut out the goldfish and paste them in the goldfish bowl.

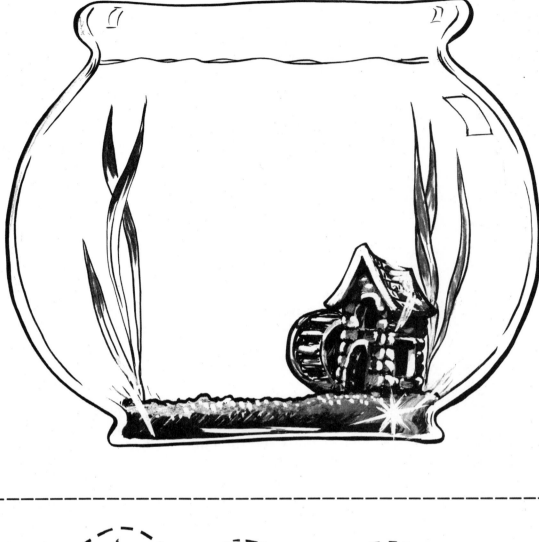

My Fish Story

Name

UNDERWATER ANIMAL BULLETIN BOARD

SEA WORLD

This bulletin board is a lot of fun for the children to create, but prepare yourself for a little mess! Cover the background with white paper. Let the children fingerpaint over the entire background in light blue; this will be the water. When the light blue fingerpaint is dry, let the children add seaweed and other plant life with shades of green fingerpaint. The seaweed may be painted separately, then cut out and stapled to the background. The children then draw things they are familiar with that live in the water - fish, crabs, lobsters, star fish, sharks, whales, goldfish, etc. Cut and paste these in the water.

Name_____

FISH LIVE IN THE WATER

Put the fish back in the water!

Draw a line from the fish to the water. Color the fish. Color the water.

- - →

- - →

- - →

- - →

- - →

- - →

UNDERWATER ANIMAL MUSIC/RHYMES

FISHING FUN

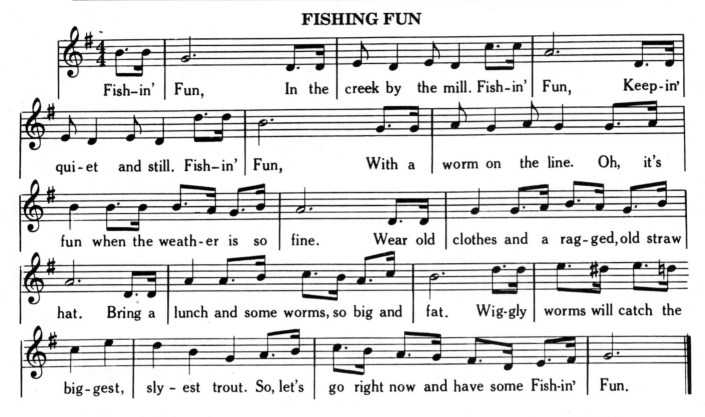

Fish-in' Fun, In the creek by the mill. Fish-in' Fun, Keep-in' qui-et and still. Fish-in' Fun, With a worm on the line. Oh, it's fun when the weath-er is so fine. Wear old clothes and a rag-ged, old straw hat. Bring a lunch and some worms, so big and fat. Wig-gly worms will catch the big-gest, sly-est trout. So, let's go right now and have some Fish-in' Fun.

OCTOPUS, OCTOPUS

Octopus, octopus, down in the sea,
How many arms can you show to me?
Only one, or will it be two?
    (show one finger, then two)
Why are all these arms on you?
Will it be three or maybe four?
    (show three, then four fingers)
Oh, dear me! Are there really more?
Will it be five, or maybe six?
    (show five, then six fingers)
I think my eyes are playing tricks.
Will it be seven or will it be eight?
    (show seven, then eight fingers)
Tell me, octopus, I cannot wait.
Octopus, octopus, down in the sea.
How many arms can you show me?
Child: "I have eight arms, as you can see."
    (show eight fingers)
(Draw a circle for the body and add eight
arms. Paint a paper sack gray and stuff it
with newspaper, tie at the neck. The add
eight crepe paper strips for arms.)

FIVE LITTLE FISHES

Five little fishes
Swimming by the bay.
The first little fish
Turned and swam away.

Four little fishes
Swimming all around.
Two left the others
Without 'ere a sound.

Two little fishes
Nibbling on their lunch.
One swam away to
Join another bunch.

The last little fish
Didn't want to roam.
So he decided
To swim slowly home.
(Make five fish and turn
into a flannel board rhyme.)

T.S. Denison & Co., Inc.   From Rhymes for Learning Times
By Louise Binder Scott
© T.S. Denison & Co., Inc.   136   *Totally Spring*

Fish Puzzle

Color the pieces of the fish.
Cut them out.
Paste the pieces together
on a sheet of paper.

This is what
the fish will
look like.

SUGGESTED READING LIST

Decker, Dorothy. *W. Stripe and the Merbear.* Dillon Press. Copyright
© 1986. *Summary:* Stripe, a little bear, dives under the sea and meets all
sorts of sea creatures while looking for the legendary Merbear.

Fish and Fables. Harper and Row. Copyright 1980. Reading Basic Plus.

Goodall, John S. *...Paddy Underwater.* Atheneum. Copyright © 1984.
Summary: Paddys underwater adventures include rescuing a small sea
monster from an octopus, meeting King Neptune, and following a pack of
mermaids to find a treasure chest.

Wegen, Ron. *Sand Castle.* Greenwillow Books. Copyright © 1977. *Summary:*
The sea creatures build a sand castle.

Yashimo, Taro. *Seashore Story.* Viking. Copyright 1967. *Summary:*
Children hear an old Japanese stroy about a fisherman who rode on a
turtle's back to a beautiful place under the sea, and then ask questions
about the story.

WARM WEATHER FUN

CONTENTS

WARM WEATHER GAMES & ACTIVITIES

MINI-BASKETBALL

The teacher or another child stands on a chair holding a hoola hoop straight out, parallel to the floor. Each child individually, or a group of children try to toss balls through the hoola hoop.

HIT THE SWINGING BALL

Hang a wiffle ball from the ceiling by a long string. A wiffle ball should be used first to ensure success and self-confidence. As the ball is swung in a pendulum fashion, the child hits it with his hand. After successfully doing this, he attempts to hit it with the wiffle ball bat. As the child becomes proficient with the bigger ball, change to the smaller ball. By altering the length of the string, the timing of the swing becomes faster and faster.

JUMPING

For some children "jumping" is an extremely easy task. For other children, the coordinated movements in the skill of jumping can be difficult. Here are some "jumping" ideas that can help to increase coordination skills.
- Holding child's hands while facing him and jumping in unison with him until the skill is mastered.
- Independent jumping on two feet.
- Pantomime of the kangaroo jump, cat jump, rabbit jump, etc.
- To jump forwards, backwards, sideways.
- To jump around the outline of a circle.
- Hopscotch using both feet.
- Jumping over small objects.
- Jumping rope games, beginning with slow movement of the rope on the ground.
- Jumping in and out of the center of disgarded tires.
- Doing spring board jumps, broad jumps, high jumps, small hurdles.

WARM WEATHER GAMES & ACTIVITIES

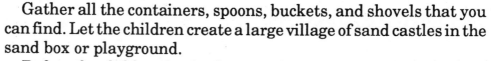

SAND CASTLES

Gather all the containers, spoons, buckets, and shovels that you can find. Let the children create a large village of sand castles in the sand box or playground.

Before the children begin their castles, give them some ideas on how to build a good sand castle. For example, they can use twigs and leaves as trees around the castle. Sand that has been moistened will be better to build with. The children will really have a lot of fun doing this activity.

GUNNY SACK RACES

Half the fun of these types of races is the falling down! Keep that in mind when you present this activity. Climbing into a bag with a good friend and being able to hop all around is hard work and a great deal of fun! You do not need to hold organized races. Simply bring the bags outside and let the children experiment with hopping inside the bags.

Before you introduce the concept of hopping with two children in a bag, make sure that you have allowed the children plenty of time to experiment with hopping alone in the bag.

COLORED CHALK DRAWINGS

During a time of the day when your school has a minimum amount of traffic in the parking lot, let the children create drawings all over the parking lot with colored chalk.

Show the children how to draw a hopscotch and how to jump on one. Draw roads and paths for the children to follow. Let the children try to draw life-size pictures of themselves. The use of colored chalk outside is a wonderful experience for a child.

SUPER DUPER ICE CREAM CONE

Color the pieces of the ice cream cone.
Cut them out.
Paste them on a piece of paper.
You will have a
SUPER DUPER ICE CREAM CONE

Make-A-List

Make a list of all the things that you can do outside on a hot day.

1. _____

2. _____

3. _____

4. _____

5. _____

6. _____

7. _____

8. _____

9. _____

10. _____

This is a good project for children to work on in a small group.

WARM WEATHER TREATS

EDIBLE NECLACES

Give each child in your classroom a piece of string. Wrap masking tape around one end of the string for a needle. Tie a knot at the other end of the string. Provide the children with a variety of round "donut-shaped" breakfast cereals for the children to string on the necklace. *(Cherrios, Apple Jacks, Friut Loops and Crackling Oat Bran are several varieties that work well.)* The children will enjoy making the necklaces but will probably have even more fun eating them!

ORANGE JULIUS

This is a refreshing drink that is fabulous for warm weather.
Put the following ingredients in a blender: 1 cup orange juice; one-half cup milk; 1/4 cup sugar; 1 teaspoon vanilla; 6 ice cubes.
Blend and serve in small paper cups.

LEMONADE

Old-fashioned lemonade just can't be beat for quenching thirst on a warm day.
Ingredients: 1 cup sugar; 1 cup water; lemon juice.
Directions: Cook sugar and water for one minute to make a syrup; for each serving, mix 3 to 4 tablespoons syrup, 1 and a half tablespoons lemon juice, and 1 cup water.

CINNAMON BITES

You will need: 1 can refrigerated biscuits; 1/4 cup margarine, melted; 3/4 cup granulated sugar; 1 tablespoon cinnamon.
What you do: Cut biscuits into quarters. Dip biscuits in melted margarine and roll in cinnamon-sugar mixture. Bake at 375° for 4 minutes. Makes 40 cinnamon bites.

Warm Weather Music/Rhymes

ROLLER SKATING

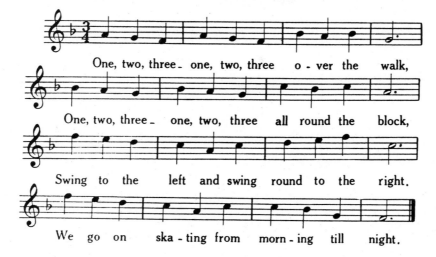

One, two, three_ one, two, three o-ver the walk,

One, two, three_ one, two, three all round the block,

Swing to the left and swing round to the right.

We go on ska-ting from morn-ing till night.

MY NEW BASEBALL

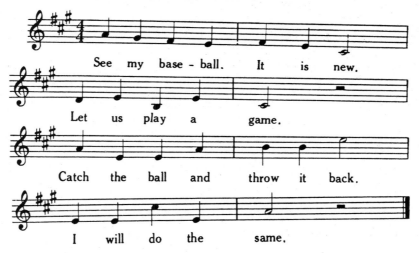

See my base-ball. It is new.

Let us play a game.

Catch the ball and throw it back.

I will do the same.

SUMMER CREATURES

A Little brown rabbit one summer day
Ran out of the burrow so she could play.
She found one cabbage that she could eat
She found two carrots and one red beet.
Out in the meadow, there were two holes;
And out of them ran two furry soft moles.
At the foot of a tree sat one little toad,
And the rabbit chased the toad all the way
   down the road.
Two squirrels sat up on the limb of a tree,
And there were two more I could hardly see.
Five field mice peeped out of their cozy small nest.
And then they ran out and joined all the rest.

They all played a game of hide and go seek
They all hid their eyes and they never did peek.
"What's that?" said the rabbit, "Out in the park.
It must be a dog. I can hear a dog bark."
The five little mice crept into their holes.
The four squirrels ran off
And so did the moles.
The rabbit ran off
And the little brown toad
Was the only one left by the side of the road.

From the book, Rhymes for Learning Times.
Written by Louise Binder Scott.
© *Copyright by the T.S. Denison & Co., Inc.*

CLOWN DAY SPECIAL ACTIVITIES

CLOWN DAY

Having a special Clown Day in the summer is a great deal of fun! Recruit help from the parents. Here are some ideas to make your Clown Day extra special fun:

1) Hang balloons from the ceiling. Tape a piece of gum to each balloon. At the end of the day each child can take home a balloon and the piece of gum.

2) Using face paints, let each child put on his/her own clown make-up. Small children do not like a lot of make-up on their faces. Nor do they usually like adults to have too much clown make-up on. *(When you have finished your make-up, be sure you still look like you!)* The children will enjoy putting on their own clown make-up and will appreciate the control of how they will choose to wear it.

3) Have the children make clown hats. A semi-circle of newsprint can be colored then folded round into a cone shape for a hat.

4) Play "pin-the-nose on the clown." The teacher (or a group of children) will need to make a large clown head and lots of noses to be pinned on.

5) Have a parade of clowns.

6) Take pictures so the children can enjoy looking at themselves again and again!

7) Read stories about clowns.

8) Show the children some pictures of some famous circus clowns.

9) Let the children draw and design some clown faces.

10) Make popcorn for a treat.

11) Let the children decorate sugar cookies to look like clown faces.

People and objects for THE BEACH
Color them and cut them out, then paste them in the beach scene.

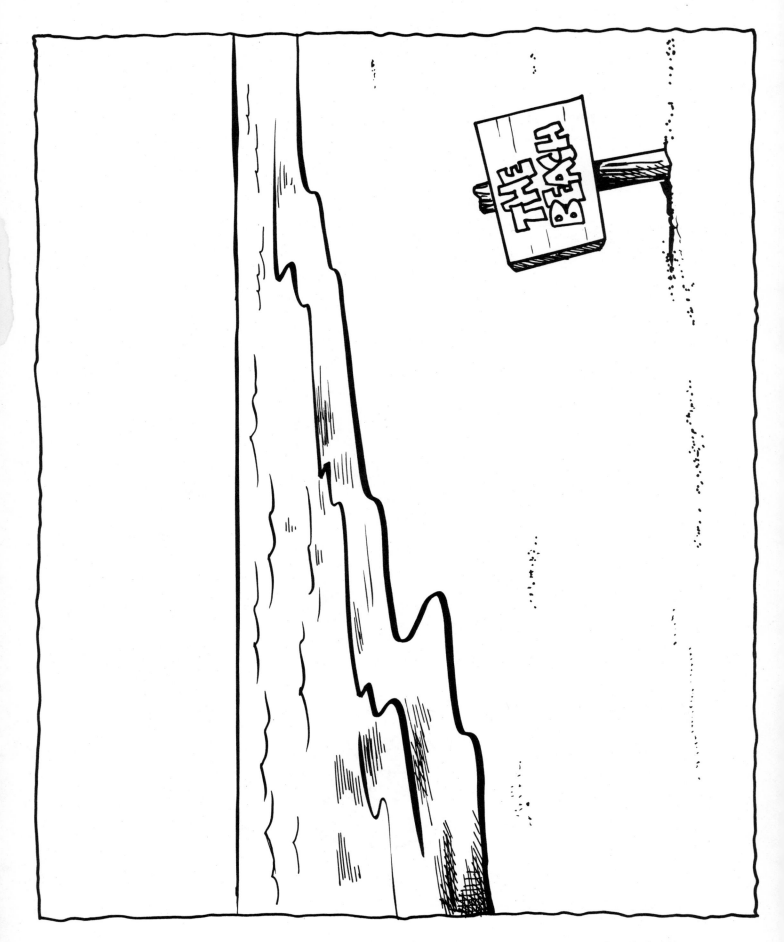

SUGGESTED READING LIST

Florian, Douglas. *A Summer Day.* Greenwillow Books. Copyright © 1988. *Summary:*A family takes a trip to the country and enjoys a summer day of relaxation and fun.

George, Lindsay Barrett. *William and Boomer.* Greenwillow Books. Copyright © 1987. *Summary:* Young William longs to swim like his new pet goose and as the summer passes he learns to do just that.

Pretlusky, Jack. *What I Did Last Summer.* Greenwillow Books. Copyright © 1984. *Summary:* A boy describes his last day of school, adventures at the beach, a neighborhood baseball game and other events of the summer.

Roth, Harold. *Summer Days.* Grossett and Dunlap. Copyright © 1986. *Summary:* Color photos and text describe children enjoying various summertime activities.

Rylant, Cynthia. *Henry and Mudge in the Green Time.* Bradbury Press. Copyright © 1987. *Summary:* For Henry and his big dog Mudge, summer means going on a picnic in the park, taking a bath under the garden hose, and going to the top of the big green hill.

Thomas, Ianthe. *Lordy, Aunt Hattie.* Harper. Copyright © 1973. *Summary:* By finding out what kind of day it is as well as what kind of day it isn't, Jeppa Lee concludes it must be summer.

MARCH

Sunday	Monday	Tuesday	Wednesday	Thursday	Friday	Saturday

T.S. Denison & Co., Inc.

Totally Spring

APRIL

Sunday	Monday	Tuesday	Wednesday	Thursday	Friday	Saturday

Totally Spring

152

T.S. Denison & Co., Inc.

MAY

Sunday	Monday	Tuesday	Wednesday	Thursday	Friday	Saturday

T.S. Denison & Co., Inc.

Totally Spring

JUNE

Sunday	Monday	Tuesday	Wednesday	Thursday	Friday	Saturday

T.S. Denison & Co., Inc.

Totally Spring

SPRING ANNOUNCEMENTS!

To _____   Date _____

_____

_____

_____

_____

_____

_____

_____

_____

_____

_____

_____

_____

_____

TEACHER

TEACHER'S NOTES